savoring childhood

PRACTICAL WISDOM FOR SLOWING DOWN

grace p. pouch

ivp

An imprint of InterVarsity Press
Downers Grove, Illinois

InterVarsity Press
P.O. Box 1400 | Downers Grove, IL 60515-1426
ivpress.com | email@ivpress.com

InterVarsity Press® is the publishing division of InterVarsity Christian Fellowship/USA®. For more information, visit intervarsity.org.

Scripture quotations, unless otherwise noted, are from the New Revised Standard Version, Updated Edition. Copyright © 2021 National Council of Churches of Christ in the United States of America. Used by permission. All rights reserved worldwide.

Scripture quotations marked MSG are taken from The Message, copyright © 1993, 2002, 2018 by Eugene H. Peterson. Used by permission of NavPress. All rights reserved. Represented by Tyndale House Publishers.

While any stories in this book are true, some names and identifying information may have been changed to protect the privacy of individuals.

The publisher cannot verify the accuracy or functionality of website URLs used in this book beyond the date of publication.

Cover design: Faceout Studio
Interior design: Jeanna Wiggins
Cover images: © asmakar / iStock via Getty Images, © chronicler101 / iStock via Getty Images
Illustrations by Charlotte Pouch

ISBN 978-1-5140-1116-4 (print) | ISBN 978-1-5140-1117-1 (digital)

Printed in the United States of America ♾

Library of Congress Cataloging-in-Publication Data
A catalog record for this book is available from the Library of Congress.

33 32 31 30 29 28 27 26 | 13 12 11 10 9 8 7 6 5 4 3 2 1

"*Savoring Childhood* by Grace P. Pouch is an excellent book with very helpful and practical suggestions for dealing with instant gratification, hurried schedules, high-speed and always-on media, rapid consuming, and growing up too fast. Parents and their children and grandchildren will be deeply blessed by this book, and so will all of us. Highly recommended as a must-read!"

Siang-Yang Tan, senior professor of clinical psychology at Fuller Theological Seminary and author of *Counseling and Psychotherapy: A Christian Perspective*

"*Savoring Childhood* reorients family life around what matters most. This book is a gift for overwhelmed parents in an unbalanced world. Grace P. Pouch creatively reimagines spiritual disciplines like simplicity, slowing, and attentive presence for everyday life together at home. Her wise insight and 'small steps' for intentional parenting offer a practical pathway toward well-paced lives of love and delight."

Rebecca Konyndyk DeYoung, author of *Glittering Vices*

"As a parent in today's fast-paced world, I am deeply grateful that Grace P. Pouch's voice exists to guide us into the ancient and timeless teachings of Christ. *Savoring Childhood* is exactly the kind of text we need: a soulful meditation on how we can teach a generation—and ourselves—to be present in the real mystery of becoming. This is a stunning and essential book."

Joseph Fasano, author of *The Magic Words*

"In our frenzied, fast-paced, attention-grabbing world, it is increasingly important for parents and caregivers to find ways to slow things down for children. Indeed, with our fully formed adult brains, we have the cognitive ability to do what our children cannot yet. When it comes to becoming tech-intentional™, this means putting skills before screens and prioritizing relationships. *Savoring Childhood* provides a guide for parents to rethink family life through a lens of slowing down, with plenty of practical and tactical strategies to do so."

Emily Cherkin, author of *The Screentime Solution*

"In this sympathetic and approachable combination of philosophy and practicality, Grace P. Pouch makes a compelling case for keeping in step with the Spirit in raising children. Challenging but accessible and actually doable, Pouch's suggestions will be life changing for both children and their parents. *Savoring Childhood* is a gift, one I wish I'd had when I was bringing up my own kids."

Richella J. Parham, author of *Mythical Me* and chair of the Renovaré board of trustees

"*Savoring Childhood* by Grace P. Pouch is a book written out of the crucible of lived experience. This makes it of enormous value, not only for our children but for us as well. There is a gentleness in the words that calls us to a deeper, fuller life of unhurried peace and power. I recommend it highly."

Richard J. Foster, author of *Celebration of Discipline* and *Streams of Living Water*

"As parents who long for a gentler pace and have worked to protect the space of childhood, we know how valuable this book is. That's why we're so grateful for Grace P. Pouch, who has gathered everyday, unhurried experiments into one resource. It's full of wisdom, simple practices, and the reminder that a slower, steadier life is still possible for kids today."

Kori Bailey and Jonathan Bailey, cofounder of the Dwell app and author of *Dwelling in Christ*

"What Grace Pouch offers to readers in this marvelous book is not only permission to give our children the gift of slowness but also rich insight and practical guidance to do it well. This is the book you didn't know you needed but are desperately glad you've found. Read it. Savor it. Ingest it. And let it help you get off the mad runaway train of soul-crushing busyness that marks our modern lives."

David and Phaedra Taylor, authors of *Prayers for the Pilgrimage*

TO CHARLOTTE AND HENRY.

God's goodness has never been sweeter

or more real to me than in the gift of you two.

Contents

Beginnings

DO YOU EVER SKIM A BOOK'S OPENING SECTION because you're short on time or in a hurry to get to parts you think will be more important?

I've done it. Probably many times. Whenever I rush through the beginning, I regret it later. Missing foundational parts of the story can make it hard to enjoy the rest of the book. Plus, beginnings can be wonderful in and of themselves. Sometimes the opening chapter of a book or the prelude to a piece of music is a masterpiece. Not just a perfunctory way to open, but a shimmering display of the artist's talent and a captivating experience you wouldn't want to miss.

This book is about a special kind of beginning. It is about the glorious opening act of human life—childhood.

God designed childhood to be an abundant, expansive season of companionship, creativity, and discovery. But that sacred season is being violated. As a book's introduction is destroyed by hurried reading, childhood is wrecked by speed.

Imagine you're a child being spun around like a top by forces beyond your control. You'd like to slow down to enjoy some of the things you see spinning by, but there is too much coming at you too fast. Living this way makes it hard to focus or find your balance. This is how it feels to be a child caught up in the frantic pace of modern life.

When kids grow up too quickly and experience life at top speed, there is little room for God in their thoughts or on their calendars. Seldom do they have enough time to play and explore, or to stay with an activity long enough to experience the sweet joy of perseverance. As a result, kids are struggling to establish roots in community, reliable morals, or any kind of relationship with God. A fast childhood is distracted, shallow, and anxious.

This crisis is present-tense, but it leads to problems down the road as well. Too many young people are reaching adulthood dizzy and bewildered about who they are and where they belong. They are spiritually and emotionally immature, unable to maintain loving relationships or handle the ups and downs of normal life.

We all sense it. Parents, grandparents, teachers, ministers, even young adults who are just emerging from adolescence can sense the precarity of childhood and can see that our pace of life has something to do with it. What pace-related problems have you been noticing?

There are many forms of speed that disrupt our lives, but I have homed in on five that I believe cause the most harm to children today:

- Instant gratification
- Hurried schedules
- High-speed, always-on media
- Rapid consuming
- Growing up too fast

These habits are deeply ingrained in our lives, but it doesn't have to be this way. We can restore a gentle pace for kids to grow deep relational roots and inner character, but we need a vision and strategies for how to get there. That's what you'll find in *Savoring Childhood: Practical Wisdom for Slowing Down*.

Together we'll consider five essential ways of slowing: Slow Gratification, Slow Schedules, Slow Media, Slow Consuming, and Slow Growing Up. We will look at how to practice each of these with our kids. And we will look at how to practice slowing down in our own lives. Parents must embrace a slower way themselves in order to help their kids have a gentler pace of life.

Perhaps I should confess before we go any farther: I don't live off the grid or anything like that, though I admire those who do. I live in a city and shop at the grocery store and worry about being on time for the carpool. And I frequently fail to live at the gentle pace of Jesus. But I am learning a better way. That way—the way of Jesus—is not a heavy burden but a light yoke, an unforced offer to recalibrate us step by step.

This book has no heroic overnight solutions. (Looking for "quick fixes" is just another symptom of our hurry-mindedness, anyway.) Instead, the suggestions I offer are small, practical ways to push back against hurry habits and unhealthy attitudes about time. They come from my family's real-life experimentation—our triumphs as well as our frustrations. I share them with you as invitations to live with greater freedom, greater connection, and greater depth. They are not really my invitations, but God's.

Whatever little corner of the world is within your effective control—your home, your classroom, your carpool, your night to have the grandkids over—no matter how small or big your influence in a child's life might be, each interaction is a golden opportunity to partner with God in creating the conditions where kids can flourish.

If we step into God's invitations to slow down childhood, we will see a resurgence of joyful young people who know themselves to be beloved children of God and who have a deep capacity to give and receive love. We'll see more children and young adults who can face challenging circumstances and respond with the character of Jesus even when it's most difficult. We'll be giving kids a better chance to live free from compulsions, anxiety, and addiction. In short, we'll be restoring the right pace for savoring childhood.

Childhood is both a beginning and more than a beginning. It is life. Life as a child.

So don't be in such a hurry that you miss its beautiful (and crucial) gifts.

HOW TO READ THIS BOOK

Every reader and every family is unique, so you and the children you love may not struggle with every form of hurry addressed on these pages. To make your reading fruitful, I suggest choosing one of these two approaches:

1. Read straight through the entire book and mark chapters that you want to return to later for in-depth practice. Ask God to highlight in your mind the areas you and your family need to work on. When you are ready for deep practice, go to a chapter and stay with it as long as you need to for the ideas to move from your head to your heart and into real expression in your life. Then turn to the next area the Holy Spirit highlights for you. Go at your own pace and in the order that suits your family's unique situation.

2. Read a chapter and pause. Before you move on, try out a practice (or a few). If possible, find someone to discuss it with you—your spouse, family, church group, or book club. Share your insights and learn from theirs. Stay with a chapter or a section while you practice for a few weeks. Once you have seen some improvement in your life and your child's life, turn to the next chapter.

At this gentle pace for reading and practicing, you may take up to half a year to process *Savoring Childhood*. That is more than fine. After all, savoring is slow work.

PART 1

Slow Gratification

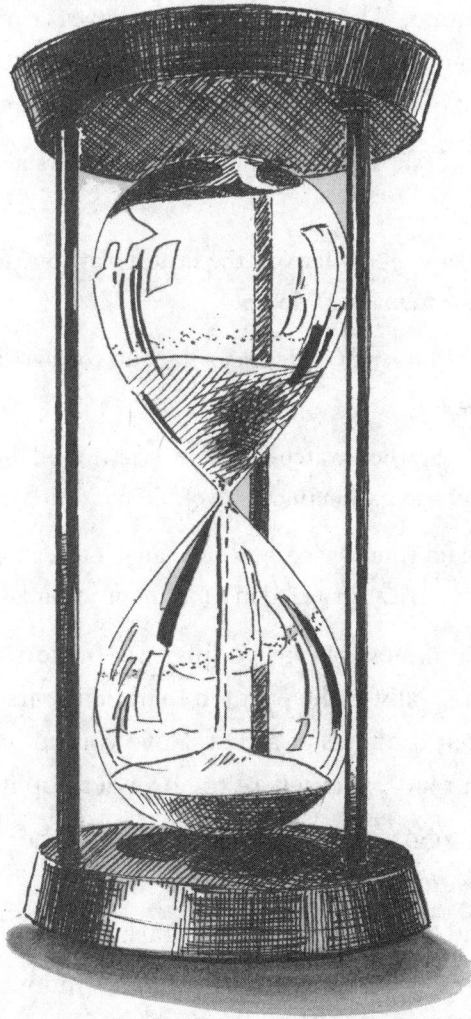

HOW HAVE THINGS BECOME more *instant* in your lifetime?

When I ask this question in group settings, we all laugh a little as we recall listening to the hiss and hum of the modem while waiting on a dial-up internet connection, watching TV shows one episode at a time with a whole week between installments, and spending months hoping a catalog order will finally arrive in the mail.

Now we feel impatient with an internet connection slower than 100 megabits per second. (The fact that we even have the phrase "megabits per second" in our vocabularies should tell us something!) And it isn't just the speed of our internet connections that has accelerated.

Someone can "dash" food or supplies to our doors at any time, day or night.

Companies compete to offer you the fastest way to reach your goals— from weight loss to master's degrees.

You can skip the line with early check-ins, and you can transfer money with a thumbprint.

Haven't we all marathon-watched a show—viewing all the episodes of a series in instant succession thanks to on-demand viewing?

Simply command your device, and you can get directions, play music, and have your queries answered in a matter of seconds.

It's wild to think how pervasive this easy-button approach to life has become, especially in the past ten to fifteen years. It might sound like paradise, but it comes at a cost. Have you noticed any of these problems in your kids, yourself, or the broader population?

- fragile or aggressive responses to even the smallest delays and inconveniences
- anxiety and avoidance in difficult tasks
- low endurance or fear of commitment (in long-term relationships, jobs, projects, etc.)
- entitlement and lack of gratitude

Speeding up the wait between *wanting* and *getting* makes our days less toilsome and more efficient, but it also stunts the growth of patience, perseverance, and self-control. These qualities, which develop slowly by God's help and our cooperation, make us people who are a blessing to be around, able to think of others, not just ourselves. And they make our contentment robust, less likely to crack when things are hard.

This is the quality of life Jesus had, and it blossomed out of the life he cultivated. Jesus came into the world through the unrushed process of developing in his mother's womb and being born, being a child, and growing up. He embraced the limitations of human existence at a particularly tough time in history. His life was rustic and slow. He walked places, worked hard to earn a living, experienced hunger and thirst, disappointment, temptation, and pain, always choosing the most loving way rather than the most expedient way.

All this non-instant, effortful living, and yet Jesus *flourished* as a human being. He savored beautiful friendships with people and with God. His words "not my will but yours be done" display his patience and his freedom from having to get his own way (Luke 22:42). People were drawn to Jesus' wise, kind, and non-anxious presence. He was fully, radiantly, responsibly alive!

This is how it can be for us, too. Richard Foster's classic *Celebration of Discipline* explores how a person can grow into the inward character and quality of life that Jesus had. Foster opens with these words: "Superficiality is the curse of our age. The doctrine of instant satisfaction is a *primary* spiritual problem." Impatience isn't a side issue when it comes to our spiritual health. It is perhaps the most pernicious barrier to that glorious earthly existence that author Rich Villodas calls "the deeply formed life."

The more we choose instant and easy, the harder it becomes to engage constructively, not to mention joyfully, in daily activities where magical, easy-button solutions don't exist. The harder it becomes to maintain friendships and family ties that take hard work and dedication. And the harder it becomes to sit with and savor one of life's slowest journeys: a gradually unfolding and ever-deepening relationship with God.

If we want our children to share in Christ's radiant aliveness, we need to help them experience *slow gratification*.

Of course, we all know that our world isn't going to revert back to slower ways. Slow gratification used to be as natural and unavoidable as waiting on the sun to come up. Now, immediacy is on tap everywhere we turn. Not only can we skip the slow stuff if we so choose, in many cases the choice has already been made for us in the products and technologies we use. In this fast gratification landscape, we need God to point us to the settings where kids can work hard and endure, collaborate and wait—so that the seeds of patience and contentment can mature and bear fruit in their lives.

I intentionally chose to make slow gratification our first stop on the *Savoring Childhood* journey because nothing is more likely to halt our progress than the illusion of instant success. Our society runs on the currency of shortcuts and "guaranteed results in three days, or your money back." That sort of mentality affects the way we approach complex issues, like the ones in this book. We want the tide to shift so that childhood is slow and wonderful . . . and we want it to shift *now*. We want things in our homes and schools to be better, and we want that change to be quick and painless. But there are no shortcuts in a child's character development and there are no overnight solutions for the problems that stand in the way of that formation. The lessons in the following chapters aren't just for our children. They are also for us, so that we will be ready for the slow work of renewal ahead.

As we root out our own impatience, we will strengthen our ability to go the distance in helping our children with theirs.

So let's begin. Freedom ahead!

1

Sweet Countdowns

"HOW LONG TILL WE GET TO THE BEACH, MOMMY?" We were about seven minutes from our driveway the first time Henry asked. He was four years old, and the two of us were headed from our home in the foothills of South Carolina down to the coast, where the rest of the family would join us at the end of the school week.

Expecting him to be disappointed that so much of the trip lay ahead of us, I framed my answer as an apology. "Sorry, buddy, but we still have more than three hours to go."

Hours and minutes were somewhat abstract to Henry's young mind, but he understood that three hours was a lot of time. Still, his little spirit was so full of excitement that he squealed with joy, "Hooray, hooray! Only three more hours till we get to the *beach*!"

His response lifted my spirits, so a short time later when he asked again, "How much longer till we get to the beach?" I cheerily reported, "Only two hours and forty-five minutes to go!"

"*Yes!*" he shouted. "We are getting closer!"

He was right. We were getting closer with every second and minute that passed. And rather than focusing on the fact that we weren't *there* yet, he was focused on our movement in a good direction—and he was actually savoring the journey. He chattered away in his car seat about things he was hoping to do when we arrived. He asked me to name every cousin, aunt, and uncle who would be there. He was looking forward to building a sandcastle and excited about what we might have for supper. As we drove, Henry was making plans in glad anticipation of his desires rather than fretting over the *not yet* of it all.

For the rest of the ride, he continued to ask for the countdown to arrival. Instead of feeling exasperated by his repetitive questions, I got more and more tickled by his enthusiasm.

Whenever we make the trek to the ocean, our family brings up this story. I suppose it reminds us that the journey can be part of the fun, even though it involves waiting. The memory holds out a glimmer of possibility: Children can learn to wait . . . even to wait with joy.

THE LOST MAGIC OF EXPECTANCY

So much effort and innovation these days goes into speeding up the journey, whether it's a literal journey to a physical destination or the journey from *I want it* to *I have it*. This pattern of instant fulfillment has a diluting effect on joy.

On a folded sheet of yellowing paper that my mom discovered among some family documents, there is an unpublished essay by my great-aunt Eugenia Pearson called "The Magic of Expectancy." Eugenia writes,

> The youthness of youth is due largely to fervent and undiluted expectancies. People begin to be old, regardless of birthdays, when they limit and tame down their expectancies. Of course they try to feel that this taming down and limitation are respectable by calling them "settling down." They seem to ignore the fact that in a living, changing, and growing world there can be no settling down at any stage of life. Expectancy keeps us in the creative livingness of life, where all desires are energized.

Eugenia was from an era of waiting stoically and not getting one's hopes up. She was a teenager during the Great Depression. To her contemporaries, she brings the message that it is good to dream big and lean into longings. It's a beautiful reminder not to give up on expecting God to do something wonderful, even when times are tough.

We are from a different era. Today, expectancy isn't dulled by having our hopes dashed constantly by hardship, but rather by having them fulfilled instantly, always. Like the character Veruca Salt in *Willy Wonka and the Chocolate Factory*, who sings, "I want the world. . . . I want it *now!*" children who habitually get what they want without delay are tyrannical when they have to wait. You see, entitlement is not expectancy. Impatience is not expectancy. Instant gratification has an unholy power to warp how our children think and feel. It muddies the clear, delicious water of expectancy and turns it into exasperation—a sour drink that makes waiting sheer misery.

Like a little devil on our shoulder, impatience whispers angry, fitful complaints in our ear that make us focus on what we don't have. But there is another way to wait. A way of waiting that focuses on what we *will* have with confidence and enthusiasm.

SLOWING IT DOWN WITH SWEET COUNTDOWNS

As tempting as it is to try to spare our kids the pain of waiting, the best way to ease their anguish is to help them discover that waiting is not so bad. My favorite strategy for shifting a child's perspective from exasperation to expectancy is to use countdowns. A countdown breaks up a long process into a series of small celebrations. This is not a trick to anesthetize or speed up delayed gratification. In fact, countdowns highlight rather than hide the reality of how far away you are from a desired destination or outcome. But by marking progress and celebrating milestones, countdowns make the journey feel endurable, even enjoyable. Children benefit from the way that countdowns place something attainable in the foreground while giving them freedom to talk about their hopes and imagine the future. Even if a desired outcome is very far away and progress is slow and gradual, stepping out the journey helps young people look forward with delight rather than despair. The journey itself is a fertile space for practicing patience and cultivating gratitude. Not everything a child wishes to attain is worth pursuing, but healthy desires deserve the space to gain momentum, even to reach the intensity of what we might call *longing*. Delayed gratification makes that crescendo possible, and makes attainment all the more sweet when it finally comes. The natural byproduct is heartfelt appreciation.

Perhaps that is why countdowns are woven into the fabric of our life together as the church. Traditionally, Christians have observed a yearly rhythm of celebrations and holy days, often preceded by a time of preparation. Take Advent, the four-week period leading up to Christmas. The traditions of Advent help us to wait expectantly for the yearly celebration of Christ's birth and to remember all of the important events leading up to it. Christians who observe Advent mark the journey in different ways: opening compartments on an Advent calendar, reading daily devotions, and lighting a series of candles to celebrate Hope, Peace, Joy, Love, and finally Christ, the Light of the World. Compared to the eons of waiting that preceded the first Christmas, this one month countdown is like the blink of an eye, but it delays our celebration long enough to help us experience some of the longing our forebears must have felt as they awaited the Messiah's birth. If we rush into the celebratory parts of Christmas without any runway, we miss out on what is actually a very *practical* way to nurture wholesome desires and genuinely thankful hearts. Instant gratification eliminates that crescendo and snuffs out its benefits.

Creating a runway also helps us enter Christmas more mindfully and responsively. At the heart of the Christmas miracle is a personal invitation: God has come to us. Will we come to him? Advent provides the space we need to contemplate that divine invitation, so that when Christmas arrives, we may respond with the exuberance of the shepherds and with the awe of the Magi.

There is one more benefit to this sweet countdown to Christmas. In the quiet waiting before the fanfare of Christmas Day, we can pay attention to the often ignored ache in our hearts for Christ to come again and set all things right. Even as we prepare to celebrate God's availability to us here and now, the countdown connects us with sensations, symbols, readings, and songs that kindle joyful expectancy for a fuller consummation than we have yet experienced. We are several minutes on our journey, with all of eternity to go!

Advent is one specific example of a countdown that people have traditionally used to extend gratification and savor the journey, and there are many others. When you were a kid, what helped you learn to wait? By pulling from the experiences that worked for you as a child, as well as from classic countdowns like Advent, you can design your own countdowns when you need a strategy to help your kids overcome instant gratification. Let's dig into a few ways this might look in your context.

HOW TO PRACTICE SWEET COUNTDOWNS

If an instant lifestyle is getting in the way of your child's ability to practice patience and savor longer processes, here are some tips for reclaiming the sweet parts of waiting.

1. ***Don't avoid telling kids about good things that are far off.*** The farther out you tell them, the longer the on-ramp for their mental preparation so that they can engage deeply and savor the experience. Of course, age is a consideration. Start with brief countdowns for toddlers (a few hours, or one day before a big occasion). And build up to extended countdowns with big kids for whom even a year or more should not be too long to sustain expectancy for something wonderful.

   A longer on-ramp also means you might have to answer eight hundred questions and risk the fallout of disappointment if something is canceled, but go ahead and tell them anyway. Shielding your kids from waiting and possible disappointment only defers the pain until they are older, and like getting your tonsils out, the older you are, the tougher the recovery.

2. ***Make the countdown tangible.*** We are sensory creatures, so lean into visual, tactile, participatory ways to mark out the steps

of a journey and energize hopeful waiting. We have digitized our lives to such a degree that invitations and calendars are often invisible to our kids. If we bring the waiting out of the shadows, we will reap the benefits of growing our children's patience.

I remember schoolteachers helping us make paper chains to count down to the end of the year. Kids can tear off one circle a day to process the movement of time and look forward with joyful expectancy. You can also make an interactive countdown to a special occasion for little ones by drawing on invitations. Draw a circle for each day from now until the big event, and let your child make a smiley face in one circle each day. Marking the time becomes something they look forward to and helps them see how many more days they have to go: "Only eight more smileys until the birthday party!"

Visual countdowns can help subdue impatience and give a sense of progress even for big kids, who are particularly overloaded with digital (intangible) modes of tracking time and events. Print and display their invitations on the fridge and keep a physical family calendar with highlights like a special sleepover, a field trip, a concert or performance.

3. *Loop kids in on preparations.* Even if a child's help actually makes life harder for you—and it will!—it forms something important in children to see themselves as contributors, and preparing can set their minds on the good that is to come with fresh energy and enthusiasm. Eventually kids who have taken part in preparations become truly helpful and enjoy it. We have finally reached that stage, and it is so rewarding!

   ▪ **Before a party:** Kids can help spruce up the house, cut flowers from the yard, and set the table. My husband's sisters always get their kids to decorate a huge homemade sign for welcome-home parties or birthday celebrations. All ages can participate in making their mark.

- **Before a trip:** Giving kids some tasks to check off turns the pre-trip into a period of joyful expectancy. With little ones, tasks can be as simple as choosing which stuffed animals to bring. Extend the countdown even more by having them choose one stuffed animal per day. "Your stuffies will be waiting to see who's next!" As our kids have gotten older, they've enjoyed drawing maps of places we're going, creating grocery lists, and helping us pack. Keep funneling energy toward getting ready for the trip to keep impatience at bay.

4. *Talk about hopes in family prayers.* When you pray aloud together, thank God for opportunities that you are looking forward to. Share your own excitement, voice your frustration when waiting is hard, and encourage kids to voice their feelings honestly. "How long, O Lord?" is a biblical plea (see Psalm 13, for example). Including God in our looking forward helps kids learn that our heavenly Father cares about all the intimate details of his children's lives. All good experiences worth waiting for are his gifts to us.

Enduring a child's many questions and emotions is a test of endurance for grown-ups. If we're honest, we could use the practice. Becoming patient is a lifelong process. So keep answering those questions, patiently and enthusiastically. Building up our own endurance helps prepare us for the long journey of shepherding young people into the childhood experiences that will help them to grow in wisdom, character, and love for God. This is the goal ahead of us, the great destination we are expectantly, or perhaps anxiously, awaiting.

"My little children," Paul wrote to the Galatians, "I am again in the pain of childbirth until Christ is formed in you" (Galatians 4:19). Long journeys, even spiritual ones, can at times be excruciating. But with every *yes* we give to God, with every step we take to cooperate with his grace, even with every chapter we read and every suggestion we put into practice, we are getting closer. (You are closer now than you were before you read this sentence!)

So hold on to joyful expectancy. And "may the God of hope fill you with all joy and peace in believing, so that you may abound in hope by the power of the Holy Spirit" (Romans 15:13).

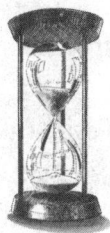

2

Stretching

I KEEP A LITTLE NOTE ON MY DESK that Henry gave me a few years back.

It says,

> would you like to play
> after your done?
> ———

I can get too caught up in work sometimes, so the note is a reminder to treasure opportunities to be with my people. To say yes, whenever I can, to their requests to spend time with me.

Another reason the note sits on my desk is because it's an artifact that represents a little parenting triumph. I can't remember now what game or activity Henry had in mind when he wrote this, but I remember that I was on a work call. Henry quietly slipped in and handed me his handwritten request. I wrote back, *Yes, but not right now. Maybe at 4:00.* And he respectfully gave me a thumbs-up.

I told Henry afterward that I was proud of him for accepting the delay graciously. This isn't always the reaction we get when telling our kids *no* or *not yet*. But we're working on it. Henry's calm acceptance of my answer that day was evidence that our approach was paying off.

Sweet Countdowns

Stretching

Time Machines

Long-Term Projects

As important as it is for me to put the kids ahead of my to-dos and say yes to their requests for my attention, it's also good for them to see me working and sticking with a task. And sometimes they need to hear me say, "Not right now." Children's development should include progressive growth in their capacity to deal calmly with delays and disappointments.

There is great freedom in not having to get your way.

OUR STRUGGLE TO SAY NO

Every person who loves a child knows that it's hard to say no. We'd rather be the fairy godmother than the one who denies a request. It's an aspect of our love—that drive to please and gratify our children's desires. But real love acts in accordance with what is good for someone, even when that means delaying or denying their requests.

We know this, and yet some of us seem to have a very tough time with tough love. The Old Testament is full of well-meaning parents who couldn't tell their children no—with disastrous results. For example, Jacob pampered his favorite son, Joseph, and didn't stop him from bragging and getting his way among his siblings. He was such a nuisance that his brothers sold him into servitude and faked his death. Thankfully, character flaws aren't irreversible, as the rest of Joseph's story proves. It's an interesting case study on the way that adversity can produce good fruit in a person's spirit, whereas overindulgence spoils it.

Overindulgence is not unique to our times, but it does seem to have gotten worse.

It is hard to say no to our kids today because, in most cases, we *could* say yes. We live in an era of disdain for moderation. And we are surrounded by "treat yourself" mantras and messages in ads, movies, and music that teach us and our kids to expect, even *demand*, satisfaction. Even though around 40 percent of US families struggle to provide basic necessities on a regular basis, children in these households hear the same messages we all do, and they see how people who live without limits are celebrated as heroes.

It's also hard to say no to our children today because we fear that restricting them in any way could induce shame. Naturally, parents who have a past history of being hurt by someone saying no in a manipulative or shaming manner may resist saying no to their own kids. We are all prone to compensate for bad experiences by going too far in the other direction. It's important for each of us to examine our personal patterns and motivations as well as the habits that circulate in the surrounding culture to see how our lifestyles promote instant gratification for our kids.

Our struggle to delay or deny children's demands is significant because instantly fulfilling their desires creates expectations that can't stand hits. Fragility ultimately makes kids less happy, less fulfilled. You can see symptoms of that inward inflexibility in tantrums, social withdrawal, and violent behavior in young people. If unchecked, these behaviors get worse in adolescence and adulthood.

Little exertions of self-will are normal and healthy. We want children to develop their opinions and preferences and learn to self-advocate. But never having to wait or hear "no" ultimately enslaves children to getting their way.

SLOWING IT DOWN WITH STRETCHING

In the Gospels we see that Jesus' freedom to do God's will and remain calm under every form of pressure and disappointment flows out of a lifetime of self-denying practice. Anyone who hopes to respond with Jesus' inward flexibility must imitate his way of formation and practice the same disciplines. "If any wish to come after me, let them deny themselves and take up their cross and follow me" (Matthew 16:24).

Especially in such a fast-gratification climate, we cannot assume that kids will just automatically develop the interior flexibility to remain calm and content when things don't go their way. "Every discipline has its corresponding freedom," explains Dallas Willard, one of the great teachers of soul formation. When we stretch our muscles before and after exercise there is some discomfort, but the corresponding freedom is greater flexibility and less likelihood of injury. When we stretch the space between our children's demands and the gratification of those demands, it brings a beautiful calmness and emotional resilience into our kids' lives.

Stretching is the practice of going just beyond a child's comfort zone before granting a request. We do it with babies learning to sleep through the night or transition from mother's milk to a cup. And we can do it with kids of all ages to push the growing edge of contentment and self-control.

We should never push back on a child's demands in a way that breaks their spirit, that crushes their God-given gift of volition. But pushing back just enough limbers them up for a world that will not always comply with their wishes and builds their capacity for life with God, where they must keep whims and appetites in check.

Stretching can be an exercise in waiting for the sake of waiting. Or it can be a way to stagger intake of something good—something fine for a child to have, but not all at once. Anyone who has weaned a child knows how tempting it is to choose temporary peace by giving in to a screaming baby, but the true and lasting peace of contentment comes by stretching out feedings and eventually substituting them with age-appropriate food. Stretching kids in other ways sets them free from enslavement to out-of-bounds appetites and prevents spiraling into anxiety and anger when plans capsize and timelines aren't met.

Sometimes stretching looks like saying no. One Christmas Eve, Henry ate what we later estimated (by counting wrappers in the trash) to be around twenty large pieces of chocolate peppermint candy. In the middle of the night—*Christmas Eve night*—he started throwing up, and he didn't feel well on Christmas Day. If I had known he was pounding the mint chocolates, I would have cut him off after five or six candies—not to be restrictive but because I don't want him to be sick! When what a child wants isn't good for him, we need to say no.

We may also need to say no for the sake of normalizing disappointment. People who can't handle not having their way or who can't say no to their bodies' urges—even when they really need to—aren't free and aren't in control of themselves. As long as you are doing it with wisdom and kindness and not to frustrate your child, you can work in the occasional "no" to strengthen a child's capacity to take it in stride.

Whether we are young or old, it is good to have some space to consider what we want. Not a "no" . . . but a "not yet." Consistent opportunities to stretch the distance between wanting something and getting it help to subdue impulsivity. Even young adults benefit from parents who encourage them to slow it down. Did you ever have to wait as a kid to attain something, and the waiting did you good? We worry that anything other than swift affirmation will sound unloving, but saying, "I don't think you two seventeen-year-olds should get married next weekend. You just met," can be a loving response. Even if your child is old enough to do something anyway without your consent, saying no or voicing disapproval means not aiding and abetting impulsivity and poor decisions.

HOW TO PRACTICE STRETCHING

Experiences of "no" and "not yet" don't have to derail our children's lives. Like Henry's thumbs-up when I told him I couldn't play right now, gracious acceptance is something kids can learn with regular practice. So let's look at a few real-life scenarios where you can practice stretching with your kids.

1. *When they want your attention.* My brother and sister-in-law have a helpful system. If one of their kids wants their attention when they're in the middle of a conversation, they reach out their hand for the child to grab. This allows the child to communicate that they're waiting to be heard and allows the adult to acknowledge that they intend to listen . . . but not right now.

Children are more likely to wait calmly if they know their request is being "held." Take age and developmental stage into consideration with how long you expect your child to wait. You can say no to some demands for attention. During a phase of wakefulness in the middle of the night, we had to say, "We're not going to come back in here tonight unless it's an emergency." We all needed rest, so saying no was for everyone's benefit.

2. ***When a request is not urgent.*** Almost every Sunday during the worship service Henry asks me for water. Even if I remind him to get it beforehand. It's not that leaving the sanctuary is completely off limits, but I want him to learn that he *can* wait. So I never say yes right away. I stretch him until the next suitable interval. "At the end of the next hymn, you can go grab a drink." Or "The sermon will be over in about fifteen minutes, and then you may go get some water." (Also a fair amount of the time I say no. He's still alive.)

3. ***When they ask for a special purchase.*** Use it as an opportunity to stretch by having your child save up money to help purchase the item. You can control the wait time and the level of difficulty involved in earning the money to make sure it fits the child's age and maturity. The interval time is a good test of whether kids really want something badly enough to spend their hard-earned cash. A note on kids earning money: At our house we distinguish between chores and money-earning jobs. Chores are just ways to contribute to the family that we all do, without being paid. Jobs are tasks beyond the usual chores that require more time and effort. These are usually kid-initiated and related to a special purchase. It's great if the work kids do is genuinely helpful, but still good for stretching their patience even if it isn't.

4. ***When they want food.*** At the risk of infuriating a whole contingent of folks with strong opinions about intuitive eating and diet culture, I want to commend gently stretching the space

between "I want" and "I get" with food in age-appropriate ways. This is absolutely not weight- or appearance-motivated, and I am not talking about counting calories or making food into the enemy. Not at all. We celebrate eating around here! I'm talking about creating enough of a waiting period for kids to think about and appreciate what they eat. (Obviously this suggestion won't work for all families and isn't appropriate in certain circumstances, but for most families who are reading this book, food is not scarce. It's overly available and too rapidly consumed, and the result is that our food intake is mindless.) You can heartily affirm a child's request for food without giving it to him instantly. For example, you can say, "I've got the goldfish in the bag, and we can have some as soon as we get there, but not right now." I remember the days when waiting a few minutes for goldfish would have absolutely wrecked my kids. I remember them falling on the floor as toddlers over the tiniest delays with food. But even though I could have padded my pockets with so many snacks that they would never feel hungry again, in the long run they needed to learn to wait ten minutes without falling apart.

It's okay to say no to some food requests. "No, you cannot have a third cupcake." Some folks worry that any "no" to food equals body-shaming, but enforcing a reasonable cutoff on cupcakes (or steak or broccoli for that matter) is just an exercise in letting enough be enough. If you have someone in your home who is super sensitive about body image, seek out a professional and modify your approach. People who grow up with restrictive and shaming food practices often swing toward one extreme or the other in the way they handle food with their kids (overly restrictive or reluctant to set reasonable limits).

5. ***Wherever you are, start there.*** Take a note from weaning: If your baby is fussy and frantic for milk at 4:40 a.m., you stretch

to 4:50. Then to 5:00. You help them to get there gradually, not all at once. And that is a truth we must apply to the way we support every form of development—for our kids and also for ourselves. If we stretch too far, too fast, we will break. As you accept the incremental nature of your children's growth in faith, character, and maturity and help children stretch, your inward calm will grow. And your patience will radiate outward to bless them and to blanket your relationships, work, and daily tasks with peace.

When waiting is frustrating and uncomfortable consider each situation the classroom of the moment, gradually setting you and your children free from having to get what you want when you want it. On the other side of momentary discomfort lies greater flexibility and freedom—for our kids and for ourselves. So may you and the children you love experience enough disruption, enough delay, enough of "no" and "not yet" to learn that you can survive. To stretch is to grow. So may you and your family find beautiful growth as you stretch to the edge of your ability. In the kingdom of God, your will and your wants do not rule. So don't let them.

People who are free from having to get their way are noticeably wonderful to be around. They are unflappable in the face of unexpected changes to their plans and focused on others more than themselves. They "have calmed and quieted [their] soul, like a weaned child with its mother" (Psalm 131:2). When we bear patience, contentment, and peace—the character of Christ—into real-life situations, it's a beautiful thing.

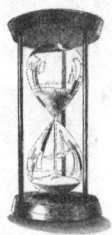

3

Time Machines

WHEN OUR DAUGHTER CHARLOTTE was about four years old, she asked us for a broom for Christmas. I thought this was a hilarious gift request, but she was completely serious. She wanted it as a realistic prop for her favorite thing to play: kitchen. She would put on her Snow White costume and bustle around singing "Whistle While You Work" while she artfully arranged toy food items on plates for us. And when she was done, she would tidy up, still humming, and put away her toy utensils with the precision and pride of a Michelin-star chef.

Fast-forward ten years, and Charlotte still enjoys playing in the kitchen—except that now she makes us real food and uses real appliances. She cooks for our family, and she makes birthday cakes and cookies on commission. Sometimes the most complicated bakes can take her an entire day, but she enjoys them and still has her whistle-while-you-work enthusiasm.

With Charlotte's prolific baking in mind, we decided we should spring for double ovens when we finally renovated our 1920s kitchen. While shopping for these new ovens, I came across something state-of-the-art in kitchen gadgetry. The most expensive ovens in the store looked exactly like their counterparts but bore a special sticker on the glass that said *Smart Oven*. The term was new to me back then, so I asked the sales clerk what made these ovens smart. He explained how they could be operated through an app on your phone and synced to voice-controlled smart home systems, like Alexa or Google Assistant.

You can just say, "Turn on the oven," and your device will execute your command.

"Ah, okay," I said, a little unsure of the value proposition here. "So . . . it saves you the time and effort of walking across the house to push the buttons?"

"Well, yeah!" he answered, as if this was clearly worth an extra five hundred dollars. "The second you want it, *poof,* it's done. Plus, people like it because it gives them a sense of control. You know—master of the house," he added with a wink.

I decided to pass.

FAST AND FRICTIONLESS

Here's the thing: I don't want anyone in my family developing "master of the house" attitudes. And I don't want my children to believe the lie that *convenience* is the ticket to a good life. Nothing sucks the whistle out of work like disdain for effort.

Childhood is naturally energetic. Picture little ones playing school, building towers with blocks, and taking care of baby dolls—have you ever noticed that they are doing *hard* work when they play? In the classroom settings where I've taught, I have always noticed the exuberance of kids as they pour their heart and soul into projects that they are passionate about. But I have been talking with parents and teachers and developmental specialists who agree that energy and enthusiasm are on the decline across a range of ages. A professor friend remarked that even at her top-tier university, many students seem dead-set on finding the easiest path to completion rather than seizing opportunities to grow. This isn't just a problem in academic settings. Fellow parents tell me that their kids have trouble *playing* creatively and energetically because they prefer passive forms of entertainment.

Is losing enthusiasm for effort an inevitable part of growing up? I don't think so. But the appetite for effort is fragile; it is easily dulled by—of all things—too much convenience. Unfortunately, the subtle idolatry of convenience that permeates our technology-obsessed culture sends kids the message that effort is a bad word. Once you give a child a shortcut (like a voice command oven) it is only a matter of time until she starts to feel disappointed with the slowness of the old way, even though she was satisfied with it just a moment ago when she didn't know the faster way existed!

Over time, losing more and more friction from childhood makes kids less able to handle challenges when they can't be avoided. What we do *off the spot* influences how we react *on the spot*. Small choices solidify into habits, which harden into strengths or weaknesses. An effort-saving gadget here and there is fine, but a childhood where everything is fast and frictionless has created a maturity crisis. A significant number of young people are reaching adulthood without the ability to make tough decisions, face challenges, or regulate their emotions. "I can't adult today" is a popular saying that you can find printed on T-shirts, bumper stickers, and wine glasses. It's meant to be a joke, but when a society's grown-ups can't consistently perform adult functions, it is no laughing matter.

What I'm trying to say is that technologies that teach kids to fear and avoid hard things are spiritual poison.

I know that sounds harsh, but listen to the words of Jesus: "The gate is wide and the road is easy that leads to destruction, and there are many who take it. For the gate is narrow and the road is hard that leads to life, and there are few who find it" (Matthew 7:13-14). Handing down a preference for convenience to our kids—through what we model and through the shortcuts we offer them—is a spiritual orientation that sets them on a path of least resistance. And that's a path that cuts corners around the difficult teachings of Jesus. Just think how *easy* it is to lose your temper, for example, or to give in to temptation, or to choose selfishness over generosity.

I want to shield my kids as much as possible from the lie that difficult things should be avoided. That's why I didn't want the smart oven. Not that someone couldn't use a smart appliance and be perfectly fine, but for me, it felt like the final snowflake in an avalanche of fast-gratification technology.

Don't get me wrong. I prefer modern living. I'm very happily not dipping a quill in ink as I write this book—although I am writing the first draft by hand (more on that later). Yes, I fantasized as an eight-year-old about living in Victorian times or in a little house on the prairie in the days of pioneers, but now that I'm an adult woman I am incredibly grateful for modern discoveries and advances in education, health, and equality. However, not *all* progress is noble or needed. Many technology "upgrades" only shave seconds off processes that, to be honest, are already easy enough. This is not innovation for the sake of a more beautiful and peaceful world. This is innovation aimed at helping you never leave the couch.

At some point, an optimistic view of technology's benefits crosses a line to become a pessimistic view of humanity and human effort. A recent advertisement directed toward parents and children begins with a father's voice addressing Gemini (Google's AI assistant tool) as if it were a human collaborator. The dad tells Gemini that his daughter plans to send a letter to her hero—Olympic track star Sydney McLaughlin-Levrone: "She wants to show Sydney some love and I am pretty good with words, but this has to be just right," he says. "So, Gemini, help my daughter write a letter telling Sydney how inspiring she is."

The ad aired during the 2024 Olympics, and it sparked so much negative feedback that Google took it down within a few days of its debut. Why the backlash from viewers? The idea that a young child's creative work wouldn't be "just right" without a robot's intervention is repulsive, for one thing. And I also think most of us feel instinctively that something precious is lost when we use technology to shortcut collaboration between parents and children.

Sidestepping collaboration to make life easier is a profound loss for childhood. But that's what most modern innovation offers: a way to work faster without relying on human (or divine) help. A reporter once asked Wendell Berry why he wrote books by hand and had his wife type them up on an old typewriter. Berry responded, "Technological innovation always requires the discarding of the 'old model.'" And in this case, Berry said, the "old model" isn't just a typewriter, "but my wife, my critic, my closest reader, my fellow worker." Innovation is reckless when it throws out human ingenuity and collaboration just for faster satisfaction.

Yes, human collaboration is hard, but it's beautiful too. In his poem "For a Student Who Used AI to Write a Paper," Professor Joseph Fasano writes,

> I know your days are precious
> on this earth.
> But what are you trying
> to be free of?
> The living? The miraculous
> task of it?

I've been letting these words echo in my mind as I reflect on the tech that we use—as a family, as a society—to accelerate tasks. It's worth asking: *What are we trying to be free of?*

SLOWING IT DOWN WITH TIME MACHINES

If you are ready to reclaim the "miraculous task" of living, and if you long for your kids to taste the heavenly sweetness of a life marked by helpfulness, patience, kindness, and creative energy, let me invite you to take advantage of time machines. Modern life is so saturated with easy-button features that to offer our kids the friction that they need, we sometimes have to journey back in time—not literally (sorry, time-travel enthusiasts!), but by being more selective about which innovations we use and when.

My family uses plenty of technology, but when we want to slow the pace of gratification for our kids (and ourselves) we sub in an old-school method or tool. These choices are our time machines, reconnecting us to gifts from the past. As I mentioned earlier, I chose to write this book by hand—at least the first draft. I think digital word processing is a fabulous innovation, but my pencil became my time machine to reach a particular set of benefits: at the pace of handwriting, my thoughts flow more naturally, I'm less worried about being perfect, and going screen-free gives me the freedom to write from anywhere without needing to charge anything. All these gifts were worth giving up the convenience of the laptop. But I returned to my computer for the later phases of the book. A time machine can be a permanent swap of modern for retro, or it can be a short experiment to revive effort, patience, or some other fruit that the more instant way stifles.

Authors Peco and Ruth Gaskovski write about time machines as a way of "unsettling assumptions about omnipresent technology use." Throwback experiences can help us realize that we don't have to adopt the latest tech trends. Our homes, classrooms, and church spaces can become alternative environments where tech is used sparingly so that children learn to discern which innovations are truly useful. Adults need that counter-formation too. Time machines teach us to respect tools we often take for granted. In fact, they knock laziness and entitlement right out of us and help us reclaim the spring in our step and the whistle on our lips.

It's important to note that the old ways aren't *always* better. So be choosy. The best time machines are those that introduce a little friction—purposefully not punitively—to slow gratification to a pace where spiritual fruits of patience, kindness, and gratitude can form:

- Chores that you can't speed up with a gadget—making the bed, walking the dog, picking up and putting away toys.
- Tools that encourage effort rather than eliminate it: a garden hose, a pair of scissors, a bicycle (the pedal kind, not an e-bike!). Even a dishwasher requires active participation by loading and unloading—which is why it's a daily chore for our kids.

- Processes that invite children to ask for help and collaborate with their peers—playing chess against a person instead of a computer, calling out spelling words to a friend rather than using online study tools, and seeking human advice rather than asking ChatGPT.

Interestingly, trends on social media and TV reveal a cultural craving, especially among today's teenagers, to revive the physicality, the attention to detail, and the sense of community fostered by old-timey processes. I think a whole generation of kids feel scammed by the instant lifestyle they've inherited. *The New York Times* reported that a group of Brooklyn teens started a Luddite Club that gets together to read physical books (not ebooks), take pictures with real cameras (not iPhones), and spend time together in person (not online). On Instagram, young people are swarming to videos like "How to serve a proper British tea"—*proper* meaning with a kettle, not a microwave or a k-cup instant-brew machine. And the hashtag #SlowLiving has more than seven million appearances on Instagram. These time machines aren't just wistful nostalgia. They are little rebellions against technologies that sacrifice beauty, tradition, and community for the sake of instant gratification. It just goes to show that kids are willing to embrace friction when it serves a higher purpose.

All these examples of savoring life's goodness are small expressions of our ultimate purpose: a radiant, with-God life, patterned after Jesus. The likelihood that the next generation will choose to say yes to Jesus' way of life depends on many factors, but one of them is surely this: Do they have a positive outlook on effortful endeavors? Or has their childhood been so easy that the thought of actively following Christ sounds just a bit too hard?

HOW TO PRACTICE TIME MACHINES

As I think about the kind of people I'm helping my children to become and their capacity to do hard things, I want to ask questions about technologies rather than just assume that we will use them. Here are some of the ways we have experimented with time machines to add helpful friction back into our family's life:

1. ***Manual labor.*** Don't worry—I'm not talking about sending kids out into the workforce! I'm talking about counterbalancing their high-tech experiences with physical tasks that aren't auto-mated. We swapped our lawn mower for an old-school manual mower that doesn't have a motor at all. You don't have to charge it or gas it up; just start pushing. It's so lightweight that both our kids can use it, and they say it is "very satisfying."

2. ***Writing by hand.*** Pencil sharpeners are practically novelty items in some settings where schoolwork is mostly done on com-puters. At home and in the classrooms where we teach, William, my husband, and I create opportunities for kids to write by hand and create physical flashcards, posters, and study aids. There's a neurological pathway from the hand to the brain that kids miss out on when they use digital shortcuts. Plus, creating ma-terials by hand is an opportunity to exercise effort, artistry, and planning skills. (Bonus: These educational time machines en-courage studying *together* with a friend or family member, which is good for social skills and rooted relationships.)

3. ***Field trips to the past.*** Our school district has a beautiful farm where several historical buildings have been preserved. Kids can visit the farm to learn what life was like two hundred years ago, try out a butter churn, and pump water from the well. We've also introduced our kids to books and movies that give them a sense of what it would have been like to live long ago. Sometimes just learning about how things used to be done can inspire kids to try a more effortful way or at least not take their conveniences for granted.

4. ***A pact to only use HI (human intelligence).*** Whether you love or hate the idea of AI, you have to acknowledge that it has the

power to shape its users' expectations about time, quality, and convenience—far more potently than any of the other technologies we have discussed so far. Personally, I don't want AI shaping my children's minds or spirits, but I wanted their buy-in on the matter. When I brought up ChatGPT for discussion at our house, the kids couldn't believe that anyone would want to outsource creative work to a machine. What would be the fun of letting a robot do the storytelling, the riddle-crafting, the birthday card design? (Oh, the wisdom of children!) If you want to keep feeding your child's intelligence and effort, I suggest talking about AI together and deciding on some boundaries.

5. *Say bye to Alexa.* (Any readers out there struggling with kids acting bossy, lazy, or entitled? If so, this tip is for you!) A smart house wired up to voice-controlled technology is robbing you of a thousand micro-opportunities to reinforce a healthy view of effort for your kids. Embodied actions—even ones as simple as physically flipping the lights on—add good friction to a child's life. Here are two reasons we don't use virtual assistants in our family:

- Appreciation simply can't grow when attainment is instant and assumed. Spoiling children is an age-old problem made terribly and unnecessarily worse by tools that deliver lightning-fast gratification without so much as a please or a thank-you.

- Even though you and I both know that machines aren't humans, AI assistants are designed to give the illusion of speaking to an entity. They have names (e.g., "Hey, Siri"). Kids form interpersonal skills and patterns of speech through their interactions and through their play. Cruel or commanding language toward pets, dolls, and toys can be an early warning sign of unkindness toward humans. So, developmentally speaking, technologies that encourage kids to practice bossing around a machine as if it were a person have a powerful training effect. They set the tone (literally) for patterns of speech and cultivate impatience with real people who don't move at the pace of machines or bend to a child's commands.

One little tip as you launch your own time machine experiments: You don't always have to divulge the *why* to your kids when you undertake a discipline for their good. If you say, "You kids need to be more patient!" they'll probably perceive it as a punishment. Instead, just say, "We're going to take a break from ____ for a while as an experiment. I'm going to do it too." Try it alongside them to show them that you're challenging yourself. After doing it for a week or so, ask them how they felt about it. Make sure they feel free to say honestly what they liked or didn't like. You can lead the way by saying, "That was hard!"

And it will be hard. That's the point. There are parts of life that will always be hard, like living in close communion with other people! But the difficulties are tied to the treasures. If children are able to participate in the "miraculous tasks" of life, our concerted efforts to cultivate effort will have paid off. A leading voice in the #slowliving movement sums up the point of embracing a less convenient lifestyle: "Savoring the hours and minutes rather than just counting them. Doing everything as well as possible, instead of as fast as possible. It's about quality over quantity in everything from work to food to parenting"—and, I would add, to being a kid.

4

Long-Term Projects

YOUR KIDDOS MUST SEE THIS! The text from a church friend included a YouTube video called "Becorns: Episode 1." In the video, David M. Bird explains that Becorns are miniature people he makes out of acorns to photograph with animals in his yard. Bird's little characters have become an internet sensation. Becorns are not quick to craft, as Bird explains in his videos. The process involves a good bit of trial and error, finding just the right twigs, feathers, and seed pods for accessories, and making multiple adjustments and repairs. Sometimes a Becorn becomes squirrel food or falls over just as the perfect photo op comes along. Despite the slow, effortful process, Bird thoroughly enjoys it. And his one and a half million Instagram followers enjoy watching.

Our son Henry was captivated by Bird's videos, but he wanted to *do*, not just watch. He made a beeline to the backyard and spent an entire afternoon foraging for materials. I was a little worried that Henry's ambition might outpace his skill. Would his growing hands have the dexterity for it? Knowing my son inherited a double dose of my temperament—big enthusiasm and big emotions when things go wrong—I wondered how this hobby would suit him. Nevertheless, Henry launched into learning the craft, and he has kept at it for the past few years. Wherever he goes, he is on the hunt for acorn caps, feathers, and curiously shaped twigs. (Our laundry rhythm now includes the extra step of emptying Henry's pockets of such treasures.)

Collecting is an exercise in patience. And that's just the prep work! Unlike most kid crafts today where all the pieces come in the box ready to assemble in three easy steps, it takes time to collect, carve, and engineer nature fragments into Becorns. I'm amazed at the amount of care Henry invests in each one—whittling a sharp point on a twig to create a tiny sword, carving a canoe out of a walnut shell, and fitting pieces together with hot glue. When little legs snap or acorn heads fall off, Henry repairs them with patient dedication.

Becorn creation takes *stick-to-it-iveness*—my mom's favorite word for not giving up. We might call it perseverance or endurance—the ability to cope and keep going even when we face setbacks. These are internal resources all of us need to engage fruitfully and joyfully in the beautiful parts of human life that aren't instant or easy. Henry's stick-to-it-iveness has grown over the past few years, I believe, as a direct result of this hobby. It offers a training space for working on something little by little for a long time and dealing with frustrations. These days he is less likely to fall to pieces emotionally, even if his creation falls to pieces literally.

DISAPPEARING CAPACITY

We're all born with a healthy portion of perseverance. Just watch a baby learning to crawl or attempting to get her thumb into her mouth. A little person's determination to try over and over and over again is a marvel! Human development depends on the strength of one's drive to keep at it. Learning to walk, tie shoes, and read; acquiring skills, forming friendships, and growing up into the character of Jesus—all of it takes endurance.

But in recent years, stick-to-it capacity has been compromised by our preference for expediency and shortcuts. It's a self-defeating cycle. Frustrated and bored by long processes, we reach for options with fewer steps and faster automation. We grow more dependent on quick fixes and short-term commitments. Eventually, tasks that feel intimidating become truly insurmountable because we cannot endure.

Children are victims of this destructive dance between our expediency addiction and the shortcuts that enable it. You've probably heard someone say that "kids these days" just can't read long books, or memorize, or build, or help around the house like they used to. That may be the case, but speeding things up to accommodate will only atrophy those endurance muscles even more. Well-meaning adults can become accidental enablers by dumbing down and shortening processes where a child's perseverance could grow.

Another reason kids are victims of disappearing opportunities to persevere is that adults themselves don't have the appetite to go the distance. I admire my parents and their generation for the energy they invested in facilitating high-quality children's activities. At our church growing up, my mom and dad led the Wednesday night program for elementary-age boys. They created challenging projects for the kids, like Disciples Care for the Homeless—an overnight experience where the boys slept outside in cardboard boxes. It was a huge effort for the kids and the adults involved. After visiting some of the bridges and tents where our city's unhoused individuals sleep, the boys had a few weeks to go door to door collecting cans of food for the rescue mission and telling neighbors what they had learned about homelessness. They also had to search behind stores for cardboard boxes they would sleep in. After much preparation, the boys and their dads set up boxes in the church yard and settled in for a long, cold night. The effort and collaboration, the searching and the discomfort were all part of the learning. Thirty years later, many of these kids still remember it as an experience that touched them deeply with God's concern for the poor.

Experiences like this have gotten harder to find. Not because kids aren't capable, but often because it's difficult to find volunteers and parents who have the creativity and dedication to support them. Instead, we settle for quick, one-day crafts that end up on the floor of the minivan and don't make a blip in a child's memory. I can sympathize with wanting an easier way. (Can't we just *buy* the cans to donate instead of going door to door?) But when grown-ups repeatedly choose shortcuts, kids lose opportunities to develop perseverance. The top spins faster, and their capacity dips lower.

SLOWING IT DOWN WITH LONG-TERM PROJECTS

While we toy with the temptation to choose the easy route, the Holy Spirit whispers the truth to us: A good life—a life that really works—is never automatic or effortless. Every goal worth pursuing requires steadily paced progress. That's why kids need to experience challenges where God can grow their capacity to stick with and savor the parts of life that aren't easy and instant.

Long-term projects take time, involve multiple steps, and require planning and problem solving. They don't have to be overtly spiritual to be wonderful classrooms for the soul. Think of a project that helped you form patience and endurance as a kid. Can you remember how it felt to work hard and to savor the fruits of your labor?

I asked some friends about childhood projects they remembered fondly, and here are a few of their answers:

- Raising animals on a farm
- Helping Grandpa build a treehouse
- Learning to tie knots at camp
- Growing vegetables
- Working a complicated puzzle
- Being in a theater production
- Earning a black belt
- Training a puppy

Notice the variety in length of time and level of skill required. Some of these were individual projects, some collaborative. They may have endpoints (like a puzzle) or be ongoing ventures with small accomplishments along the way (like raising animals). What these projects have in common is that they defy instant gratification. They require hard work. And yet, whenever I ask people about the long-term projects of their childhood, joy bubbles up as they share memories with me. Isn't that interesting? We think we spare kids from drudgery by eliminating slow, difficult processes from their lives. But every person I have asked, "How did it feel to work hard?" recalls feeling joy, pride, and camaraderie through these endeavors.

Long-term projects are golden opportunities because they do uncomfortable work in our children's spirits while satisfying deep, God-given desires. They swap cheap gratification for true spiritual fulfillment. They foster close collaboration, a sense of usefulness in doing good work, and self-confidence in finding that they can keep going.

The most fulfilling and also the longest of all life's projects is our walk with God. A relationship with the Lord is not something we choose one day and then check off the list; it is never-ending! Jesus says that being with him and becoming like him is a "daily" process of trust and training (Luke 9:23). Eugene Peterson's classic book *A Long Obedience in the Same Direction* describes this reality, and it has a brilliant subtitle: *Discipleship in an Instant Society*. Peterson recognized that effortless living weakens the soul for life's most important endeavor. Unless we counter instant gratification with slow and effortful projects, our children's discipleship is likely to be derailed—not by losing faith, but simply by losing steam.

Long-term projects enrich childhood. They give kids the chance to taste the sweet harvest of long-awaited goals and to lean into a friendship with God that is not static, but ever-deepening and unfolding. And long-term projects in childhood also enrich adulthood. They are a way to begin building today what your child will need for tomorrow's commitments—job, friendship, marriage, church, parenting, and a "long obedience" in the way of Jesus.

HOW TO PRACTICE LONG-TERM PROJECTS

So what are the right projects for your child, student, or grandchild? The most effective long-term projects to invite our children into are those that bring them joy as they patiently persist in their work. That means helping kids choose projects that complement their unique personalities, interests, and developmental needs.

A great place to start is outdoors. The natural world has endless opportunities to stretch a child's perseverance while bringing great delight. A teacher friend recently helped her kindergarteners create an entire classroom in the woods behind their school—with seats and play areas and a little garden. Each child contributed to the development of the space over the course of an entire school year.

On a smaller scale, my son Henry and my nephew Charlie worked together to build a fort made of sticks under a tree in their grandparents' yard over the course of five weekends and then invited the whole family to see their creation. Some nature projects train kids in delayed gratification, like planting bulbs they won't see bloom for several months. Others are opportunities to stick with a single activity and push through boredom, like spending a whole afternoon digging tide pools for hermit crabs or picking dandelions and weaving them into crowns.

I was curious what other sorts of long-term projects my kids might recommend. Henry suggested going fishing (he knows from experience that fishing takes persistence), working up to a black belt in taekwondo, and building a model spaceship. My daughter Charlotte suggested baking and decorating a cake, learning to play piano, and reading through a series of books—all projects she has found personally satisfying. A child's buy-in and sense of ownership are essential. Kids can show remarkable initiative, creativity, and persistence when we allow them a reasonable degree of freedom to pursue activities that genuinely interest them.

Once your children have some long-term projects in mind, it is important to think through how you can support them in sticking with it. You may be wondering, *Is it ever okay to let a child give up? When and how much should I help?* These are very important questions. Allow me to respond with a resounding *it depends.* A child's preferences, maturity level, and gifts will influence the answers. Also I encourage you to discuss your questions with friends and family as you continue reading. God has given us each other as a great source of wisdom.

Here are some wise principles that our family has picked up and put into practice:

1. ***The right project for the right age.*** For little ones, twenty minutes can be a *very* long time. At this stage, a long-term project might look like working an age-appropriate puzzle or developing a piece of art over several short sessions. Older kids who expect activities to be finished in a snap may need to start small. Gradually extend the finish line to help them build up to a healthy level of endurance.

2. ***Assist (but not too much).*** A little assistance—on the front end or at very difficult points in the process—can help a child endure longer and do better-quality independent work. Know yourself as a parent or teacher; if you're prone to helping too much and solving problems for your child, you need to let them wrestle through it more. If you're more likely to be hands off, try engaging more. Gentle assistance and collaboration teach your child to graciously receive help and work well with others.

3. ***Make it a privilege, not a punishment.*** Kids will have intrinsic motivation to stick with a long project if it is something they consider worthwhile, and even more so if they think it is a special privilege. So let them stretch their wings! If they show an interest in cooking a meal for the family, let them experiment. If they want to create a musical for their church choir, or build a model car, or plan a camping trip, give them the opportunity to take risks, and they will savor the process even as it challenges them. This is especially important for teenagers. There will always be tasks and projects children don't enjoy that still need to be done, but make sure they have ample opportunities to dive into projects they are naturally drawn to. Those are great

training grounds for developing stick-to-it muscles they will use elsewhere.

4. ***When a child is discouraged.*** Resist the urge to swoop in and solve everything or halt the project. Kids' capacity to recover from setbacks will amaze you. And when they solve something themselves it forms a healthy sense of pride. Each situation is different, however, so take the approach that fits your child and *acknowledge that it's hard.* Just knowing that someone sees their effort and knows it isn't easy can bring kids fresh energy to stick with it.

- **Praise progress, not perfection.** When Henry decided to make Becorns, I knew he wouldn't be able to make them with the same expertise as David M. Bird, but what mattered is that he did it with the best ten-year-old effort and skill he could muster. Long-term projects are about small steps in the right direction, not instant success. Perfectionism is *anti-*perseverance because it discounts progress. If perfectionism rears its head, take some time to describe the progress you see to help your discouraged child feel proud of age-appropriate accomplishments.

- **Look for inspiration.** Watch a cooking show with your as-piring chef or give them a cooking demonstration. Let students in the yellow belt class at taekwondo watch the black belt kids practice to catch a vision of where their hard work will take them. When spirits get low and the road feels long, giving kids a bird's-eye view of where they're going revives their interest.

- **Create off-ramps that don't feel like failure.** Not every project is the right fit, and kids will have a better attitude about experimenting if you don't always force them to finish. We once signed up for a swim team that our kids really didn't want to do. We said, "Let's go to the practices for a week and see what you think of it." When the week was over, we could see that they weren't enjoying the swim team at all. So we told the kids we were proud of them for giving it a try and allowed them to stop there.

■ **Remember the goal is life.** The aim is to help our children live well, respond wisely, and enjoy God's good gifts. So if a project isn't bringing life, let it go.

5. Celebrate!

■ **Milestones** divide up a long-term project into steps so that progress is more visible. Programs with badges and ceremonies have the right idea: Celebrate reaching point A, then point B, then point C.

■ **Let kids show and tell** when they reach the end of an intense project. Listen well as children share so that they sense your interest and appreciation for their hard work. Even big kids like to see their report card on the fridge or have grandparents cheer them on at the school play.

■ **Remember to say how proud you are.** Words of affirmation (and hugs!) are important ways to celebrate growth, and they help tune a child's ear to the Spirit's inward affirmations: *Well done, good and faithful servant.*

A last word of encouragement: If you're reading this book, you're already involved in a wonderfully rewarding long-term project—caring for a child! So hang in there. Don't try to shortcut the hard parts. Keep the long-range view in mind. Every once in a while, step back and admire the people you're helping to raise.

PART 2

Slow Schedules

I'M WRITING THIS FROM A BENCH at the YMCA. On the field beside me, my ten-year-old son is playing flag football.

I feel calm. We made it here tonight without rushing. For various reasons, we missed the previous two practices and a game. And you know what? Missing out was fine. The YMCA understands its place on a family's calendar. It doesn't make bold claims like, "This team comes first, ahead of everything else." You sign your kid up, you pay, and then you show up when you can.

Show up when you can—doesn't that sound like a gracious way to conduct an extracurricular program?

Readers with a strong sports ethic might think I'm trying to pick a fight here. Please forgive me. I understand the importance of commitment and team spirit and giving it your all. But flag football for ten-year-olds is not the Olympics. It's low key and accommodating, and at this stage of our family's life, that's what we need.

I know I'm not the only one looking for some relief from the tyranny of an overbearing schedule. Part two of *Savoring Childhood* barely needs an introduction. Whenever I bring up the question "What's preventing kids from savoring childhood?" the first responses are always calendar-related:

- Our family has no margin or downtime.
- We are always rushing and running late.
- It's like we are passing each other coming and going. We barely see one another.
- My kids are exhausted.

Savoring childhood isn't *just* about slow schedules. But a disordered schedule is a thug we can't ignore.

The activities that fill our days and weeks are not bad things. Many of them are essential things. But to the extent that we let them strong-arm their way into the driver's seat and speed us through life, our lives and our children's lives suffer. If we lose control over what makes the list, *the list makes us*—it makes us anxious, scattered, overcommitted.

It robs us of opportunities to know each other at the deepest level and to enjoy life to the full.

This is the opposite of how God wants our children to live. If a fast schedule is something you struggle with, take a moment of quiet and consider this question prayerfully: Why do we let our schedules run us ragged?

I think often we are scared that we will miss out on valuable experiences and connections if we scratch something off the calendar. We might feel anxious about what others will think of us. Deep down, we may be afraid of not doing or being enough. Or maybe it's just that being busy is so normal for us that when we experience a lull—a weekend with no plans, for example—we feel antsy and dissatisfied. In many cases, we know that our family schedules are a source of stress and we want things to change, but we feel trapped in a pattern that is beyond our control.

Whatever the reasons for our chronically fast schedules, the Lord can give us wisdom to set boundaries that will keep us on a good path at a sustainable pace.

The chapters ahead are *not* a guide for how to be more functionally busy. I am not going to teach you how to color-code your calendar and get up at 4:00 a.m. and drink power smoothies so that you can increase productivity and fit more things into your day. Instead, I invite you to join me in taking stock of your time.

If your days are a blur of fast-paced activity . . .

If the most important relationships get too little of your best attention . . .

If your children don't have energy to savor wholesome activities, blank space to be bored, or time off to rest . . .

Then I don't think your problem is motivation or organization. My invitation to you in the chapters ahead is to do less. I know that isn't the answer we typically want to hear. We want the secret sauce for how to do it all *and* be perfectly rested and connected. I'm afraid that doesn't exist. A gentle pace means missing out on some things, even disappointing someone at some point—maybe your teammates or your friends or yourself.

Whenever I feel worried about not being able to do it all, I try to remember that Jesus also faced the limits of being bound to a certain time and place with human needs and competing invitations. During his earthly life he was like us, unable to be in two places at once. Everyone wanted a piece of him. And he didn't comply with every invitation. Herod, for example, "tried to see him" but couldn't get Jesus on his calendar, despite being a celebrity (Luke 9:9). Jesus' priorities were guided by his Father. "For I have come down from heaven not to do my own will but the will of him who sent me" (John 6:38).

It's a tough example to follow. My will gets in the way. A *lot*. I'm tempted every day to squeeze more into the schedule than I should. Requests related to "being a good mom" are especially enticing. Go out for every volunteer thing, enroll the kids in every enriching activity, never miss an opportunity. But that is a recipe for burnout. And if we do all of those things, when will we actually savor life together? When will we have time for little things, like helping her kick up to a handstand (for the hundredth time), or reading *The Hobbit* together after bath time, or sitting on a bench at the YMCA watching kids' flag football as the smell of fresh-cut grass floats on the breeze?

Maybe you've felt that tug-of-war too. On one side, expectations and pressures to keep up. On the other side, a gentle pace of life. What you put on your schedule is a decision for you to make with God, taking into consideration your unique circumstances and relationships. But here are two guiding principles that apply to all of us:

- A schedule guided by God will never pull us away from him.
- The overflow of a well-ordered schedule is greater love—for God, for others, and for ourselves, limits and all.

In a God-ordered schedule, we will find ourselves both more reliant on him than ever to accomplish anything worthwhile, and less burdened than ever because we will have let go of things we are not called or equipped to do. Listen for God's invitations, and *do as you can*. That will be enough.

5

A Palace in Time

AN OVERNIGHT SLEET-RAIN MIX had made the roads in our Southern town impassable. So our little church sent out the message to stay home and stay warm. On this particular Sunday, the unexpected cancellation was what my soul needed. Instead of rushing around to get dressed and get out the door, we stayed in our bathrobes. We ate an unhurried breakfast of pancakes. And then the kids (ages seven and ten at the time) prepared a homemade worship service for the four of us. I had suggested they might like to play church this morning and dress up like pastors. They were thrilled.

Using their best energy and effort, they crafted a liturgy consisting of a reading from their children's Bible, a sermon (handwritten reflection on the Bible story), a time for spontaneous prayers, and music from the old Baptist hymnal we had at home. They scrounged up candles and a decorative cross from the bookshelf and would have had a lovely altar on the upholstered ottoman had I not intervened due to a leaning candle. A red scarf served as a stole over Charlotte's nightgown. And Henry found the microphone in the dress-up box for that modern church effect as he announced our music. He had marked close to thirty hymns with sticky notes, including his favorite, "Holy, Holy, Holy." (I intervened once more to suggest he narrow his selections down to a top five.)

The service began. It was simple and pure. We were lifted by the children's praise and an unexpected break from our typical Sunday routine. All other concerns, all other tasks, were set aside. Partly by necessity—we couldn't go anywhere, anyway. And partly by choice—to savor the rare beauty of the icy day and this sweet time together. It was a perfect reorientation for me, a reminder of why I need days off from focusing so intensely on doing, earning, and achieving.

FAST SCHEDULES AND OUR SCARCITY MINDSET

Doing, earning, and achieving. These are the concerns that fuel our schedules most of the time. Some of that is normal. We have to survive! But our tendency is to focus on what we don't have, and to believe that there isn't enough time to get it all done.

Little children do not worry about these things the way that we do. They don't start the day fearful about checking off to-dos. Kids barely keep track of what day it is, much less what hour. And they naturally inhabit each present moment with gusto, unconcerned about how quickly it will slip away. Time is full for kids, not scarce. Can you remember how it felt to be a child, free and filled with wonder? Soaking up each present moment without feeling pressed by responsibilities to accumulate, control, and accomplish?

It's a glorious freedom that we all long for. And it's a freedom God longs to give us.

After God liberated the Hebrew people from enslavement in Egypt, he designed the Sabbath to set them free from the mindset they had acquired under the strain of constant labor and scarcity. This day was to be their training space for trust, their reorientation to a life of provision and close communion with the Lord. God laid out the plan: once a week they were to cease their normal striving and be in the world as children are—dependent, grateful, not preoccupied by business. "'Six days shall work be done, but the seventh day is a Sabbath of complete rest, a holy convocation; you shall do no work: it is a Sabbath to the LORD throughout your settlements'" (Leviticus 23:3).

To trust God more than money and accomplishments feels risky. And that's the point. Sabbath invites anxious people to take the risk and see that the world does not stop turning when they set aside their work. The unholy hunger for accumulation is transformed into desire for God's presence, and distorted ideas about what is needed can come into alignment with God's reality.

This is an extremely important lesson for us grown-ups—a corrective to our silly ideas about scarcity and our overblown sense of self-reliance. And it's a practice that protects our children's naturally healthy outlook about time and their childlike trust in the heavenly Father from being corrupted by a schedule that never stops.

The way modern Christians typically think about and practice the ancient commandment is so diminished. It's sabbath chopped off at the knees and hammered down into a tiny one- to two-hour box of attendance at a service, when our souls deserve so much more. Instead of subsisting on these crumbs of sabbath, God wants us and our children to slow down and savor the great banquet he has prepared.

SLOWING IT DOWN WITH A PALACE IN TIME

To place God at the center of our lives and have his values and his sense of time shape our own, we need regular and deep experiences of sabbath. This is hard for families to do, but not impossible! An illustration that has profoundly shaped my family's approach to sabbath is Rabbi Abraham Heschel's phrase "a palace in time." Into the rhythm of every seven-day week God has woven a palatial twenty-four hours that is meant to be free from everyday pressures so that it can be full of intimate connections and delightful, reorienting experiences. It interrupts the flow of our fast-paced schedules that press us toward output and acquisition. And like a precious portal, it leads us out of the hustle to return us to the childhood freedom of just being alive and enjoying the gifts of God.

I haven't been to many real palaces, but I know that they are well-fortified. What they keep out is part of what makes them safe and special. It is the same with sabbath. We get into it by keeping things out of it. As natural as it is for kids to live freely and lightly, they also absorb our family perspectives about time, and they can vicariously experience our worry, rush, labor, or laziness. The palace principle— that we must bar the door against certain intrusions to experience the delights within—has given me helpful clues for how to modify the family's schedule in a way that connects kids to the blessings of sabbath.

Deciding that certain activities are off limits for ourselves and our kids on the Sabbath is not a punishment. Not a show of piety. Not even countercultural bravado. The palace boundaries preserve our children's freedom. We learn this way of parenting from our heavenly Father, whose rules are always purposeful, always *for* us. Jesus says it this way: "The Sabbath was made for humankind and not humankind for the Sabbath" (Mark 2:27). If there is anything that monopolizes your child's attention or subtly sends them the message that their worth is based on their accomplishments, the boundaries of the palace are a way to say, *This is not the center of our lives; Jesus Christ is the center of our lives.*

Sometimes, pausing something like mind-numbing entertainment or a high-pressure hobby for one day can help us realize that we need to permanently delete it from the family schedule. Other times, we pause simply for moderation and refocusing. A bride and groom on their wedding day don't mow the grass or go into the office. Not because mowing and work are *bad*. They are simply the kinds of activities to put on hold so that a couple can enjoy a palatial moment in their lives. In the same way, we pause certain activities in order to clear out the hours of the Sabbath "so that *something of value* can inhabit them."

What is "something of value" that is hard to come by—for you or for your kids—in the course of a normal day? Maybe it's sleep. Maybe it's a rich conversation with a parent or friend—uninterrupted by to-dos and appointments. Maybe it is the freedom to unfurl your beautiful body from its work-cramped stasis, to walk and stretch, to sink your toes into grass, water, or sand. Maybe your family's screen-bleary eyes need time to look around with no agenda—to watch the robins pecking for worms, to admire the clouds, to "consider the lilies" (Matthew 6:28).

Are any of these things spectacular? We don't seem to think so when we rush past them each day without a second glance. But in the light of sabbath's slow gaze, we recognize that this is beauty our souls were meant to stand back and celebrate! If God used his "day off" to enjoy the world he created, it is only fitting that we spend time admiring nature on the Sabbath too. When we do so, we are flooded with delight and gratitude for the Creator.

Truth is another "something of value" that God wants us to encounter in the palace in time. Sabbath creates an unpreoccupied space for the voice of God—on the pages of Scripture, on the lips of the pastor, in the whisper of the Spirit—to reach the ear of our heart. Children are naturally hungry for truth, if we can clear aside the many distractions that often prevent them from deep encounters with God's sources of revelation.

The architecture of Sabbath was also designed to bring us together as the community of faith. Scripture echoes with the reminder that the Sabbath is a day for *sacred assembly*. Fellowship can be challenging, messy even. But congregating as a community gives us and our children a sense of belonging and companionship, and it is something the palace in time clears the schedule to accommodate.

At the center of these gifts—freedom, nature, truth, community—is the Lord, the giver of all. In the biblical account of creation, God takes a restful sabbath to enjoy the results of his labor. He isn't recharging (this isn't necessary for God); he is resting for the sake of *savoring*.

We join God in the palace of rest to savor alongside him. Our enjoyment becomes an offering to the One who makes it all possible, and he receives the gratitude that bubbles forth from our hearts and lips. This is the essence of worship, the holiest and highest of activities we undertake within the time palace, and the one activity that we will continue to do forever and ever, even when this earthly life is over.

Helping children enter the palace in time is foundational because it is one of the primary places where they can taste and see that God is good. The idea that kids are fully capable of savoring God and his gifts and engaging in the holy work of worship might sound saccharine or a little far-fetched, but Jesus pierced the doubt of his contemporaries on the subject with this question: "Have you never read, 'Out of the mouth of babes and nursing infants You have perfected praise'?" (Matthew 21:16 NKJV). Children are more than capable of participating in worship and even facilitating it, as my kids reminded me on that icy Sunday morning of child-led worship.

The author and perfecter of how to savor the delights of the palace in time is, of course, Jesus. If we could go back in time to observe his sabbath practice, we would see him honoring the boundaries that God laid out long ago to protect the day of rest for soul-nourishing, God-centered activities. The Gospels give us glimpses of Jesus on the Sabbath, joining in Scripture readings and prayer with his community. We see him walking through fields with his friends, close to creation and the truths that it reveals about the Creator. We see him participating in rituals that remember God's salvation—the Passover and other festivals, where food, fellowship, and celebration make space for deep remembering and expressions of gratitude. And we see Jesus comforting, healing, teaching, and extending compassion on the Sabbath, so as to embody the unceasing, unresting, ever-working nature of God's love.

Jesus shows us that all sabbath graces emanate from and return us to God. Sabbath is not about "feeling good" to please ourselves, but it is deeply fulfilling. It makes space for renewal, reconnection, worship—the kind of communion that feeds the soul with "righteousness and peace and joy in the Holy Spirit" (Romans 14:17). "Sabbath is not an interlude but the climax of living," awakening us to the divine potential of every day and every moment to be a meeting place with God.

HOW TO PRACTICE A PALACE IN TIME

It falls to us—the schedule makers—to create the conditions for sabbath. We cannot force our children to worship, trust, or praise the Lord. Nor should we try! But we can build our family schedules around sabbath to offer our kids the freedom that the palace makes possible and to offer them ourselves—rested, centered on Jesus, and overflowing with grace. As our kids experience the palace principle (that keeping certain things out helps us to enjoy the Lord and his gifts) they are learning essential skills for abiding in God's presence always and forever.

These three steps can help you plan a sabbath for yourself and the children in your care:

- *Choose a day.* To give children enough time to reconnect with God and the world in a reorienting way, choose a twenty-four-hour period of time to step away from normal rhythms. The traditional *shabbat* is Saturday. God set apart the last day of the week for the ancient Hebrew people to rest. There is something beautiful about sabbath as the culmination of the work week. Modern religious Jews and some Christians continue to practice sabbath on Saturday. For Christians, Sunday became the standard sabbath day because it was on this day that Jesus rose from the grave. There is something beautiful about placing a palace in time at the beginning of the week because, from a slow-schedule perspective, it sets a pace and tone that orient the week ahead. Kids can benefit from a palace in time any day of the week, but doing it on Saturday or Sunday joins your family with a community of others, and that's helpful precisely because slowing down is already such an upstream slog, culturally. It's good to have friends who share your values.

- *Set your intentions.* What will you keep out and keep in the palace for the sake of your child? The following prompts can help you form a plan and stick to it. (This exercise works best when we listen for God's nudge and make choices with his guidance.):

I will / we will clear away (or let go of) _____ *(something true of a regular day's "grind"—commitments that consume your focus and energy, especially related to money-making and personal accomplishments)* **to make space for** _____ *(something soul-nourishing, God-honoring, beautiful).*

- *Make it a weekly routine.* By God's design, the more regularly you practice it, the more this different way of experiencing time can shift your outlook and transform your life.

As children get older, there comes a point when they should make their own decisions about their calendar, and of course about their faith. If a child begins to question or resist sabbath practices, connect them to the beauty of God's design and draw them into the *why* behind it. This may not convince them, but showing young people a beautiful alternative to the world's hustle culture and its values of doing, earning, and achieving might resonate with their deepest longings. Meanwhile, a family schedule can uphold boundaries for the good of everyone who lives under the same roof—including the parameters that protect the palace in time.

As you experiment with a palace in time, keep a lookout for things that limit kids' freedom to savor or that draw them back into worries and ambitions. Is anything trying to push its way back into your life or your child's life that doesn't belong in the palace?

If so, that may indicate that an even longer break would be helpful. You can extend the palace's boundaries into other parts of the week wherever you want to connect children with sabbath's gifts. Here are a few options:

1. *Mini sabbaths.* Use small pauses to reconnect to the truths about time we've discussed in this chapter.

- Take an afternoon (or a few afternoons) off with the kids. "We need a break from swim lessons this week. Let's just rest and enjoy some time in the backyard together."

- Set aside twenty minutes of quiet time during the day for prayer, nature-gazing, or another delightful form of rest.

2. *Sabbaticals.* Widen the clearing on your schedule beyond one day to sink deeper into the riches of the palace.

- **Camp** can be sabbath-like for children if it has the right ingredients: time away from rigorous work and pressures to achieve; freedom from technology and other things that pull them away from engaging in the joys of the present moment; and the gifts of nature, fellowship, and corporate worship.

- **Spiritual retreats (for adults or youth).** Whether solitary or with a group, guided or self-led, retreats can be a time to reconnect with beauty and goodness in a way that guides our thoughts toward God and launches us into worship.

- **A seasonal pause** from certain things in order to enrich your engagement with God—maybe a formal sabbatical from work or an informal break from certain commitments. Try giving kids summers off from school and high-pressure sports, music, or other accomplishment-oriented activities. Allowing kids to play for fun without the rigor of lessons and competitions is an important form of sabbath in childhood.

BUT SERIOUSLY, CAN PARENTS REALLY HAVE A SABBATH?

We've been talking about carving out a palace in time where the hard work of normal days is set aside so that we can take refreshment and delight in the Lord. Sounds great, but let's be real. If I have little kids, pausing from work isn't really an option. Can parents and caregivers actually have sabbath?

Absolutely.

God's instruction to do no work on the Sabbath does not mean ceasing all effort. If it did, we'd have to pause from walking, brushing our teeth, pushing a stroller, preparing bottles, and so on. Historically, there have been folks who took sabbath restrictions too far. They thought that all effort on the Sabbath was against the rules, except for the work of worship (singing, praying, etc.).

But this is not what Jesus modeled. Jesus shocked his peers by healing and performing miracles on the Sabbath, which is pretty big work. The Sabbath watchdogs were sure he had offended God with his *effortful* kindness. But Jesus countered them by explaining that actively caring for those whom we are in a position to help brings glory to God. God is always, always working for good in the world (John 5:17). Acts of kindness and care, therefore, are not at odds with sabbath's goals. In fact, they are integral to the palace in time.

This is good news, because it won't be possible in certain seasons of our lives to take a whole twenty-four hours off from the duties of caregiving. Caring for children is extremely demanding. It can direct (and even consume) our focus, strain our backs, and drain our energy. But it is not a self-centered effort. It honors God. Jesus affirmed this when he voiced God's perspective on caring for anyone—whether young or old: "Truly I tell you, just as you did it to one of the least of these brothers and sisters of mine, you did it to me" (Matthew 25:40).

In seasons of life where the labors of love are unavoidably intense, we need to let God help us reimagine what sabbath can be. Modify and do as you can, not as you can't. Here are some tips for caregivers struggling to experience a palace in time:

- If someone at church can lend a hand by playing with your kids for a bit, take the help and enjoy a temporary break from rocking your colicky infant or singing "The Wheels on the Bus" to your insistent toddler.

- When you are caregiving on the Sabbath, avoid unnecessary intrusions like scrolling social media that turn your thoughts elsewhere toward other goals. Let your child be the center of your attention. Loving your child is a way to love the Lord.

- Dwell on the glory that lies hidden in the small and ordinary. Watching a baby play with something might not sound as grand as studying the wonders of the universe, but it is! Just watch! Watch with fresh eyes. As you watch this little human, let the laughter and amazement that bubbles up in you become your praise to God.

- Sense God with you, strengthening you and caring for you as you do things that are tedious for the sake of someone you love. If sensing God's presence is hard (I get it; he's invisible!), try using some props. In the Old Testament, God's people used incense, fire, and a tabernacle full of sights and sounds to represent the presence of the Holy One in their midst. As you care for little ones on the Sabbath, keep something nearby that you can smell, see, or hear—like a candle, some flowers, or soft music—to help you to remember that God is with you in your caregiving and will supply all the loving energy you need.

- If we didn't have such hurried Saturdays (the true week-end) we could start the week with a more palatial sabbath rest. If you're able to not work on Saturday, make that your time for catching up on errands, social calls, and pure relaxation so that Sundays can be slow and soul nourishing.

I know it isn't restful when the children are small. It doesn't feel very much like a palace. But time together—for them and for you—is more precious than gold.

This blessing, given to the very first people God asked to set apart the Sabbath, is also for you and the young people you love:

The LORD bless you
  and keep you;

the Lord make his face shine on you
    and be gracious to you;
the Lord turn his face toward you
    and give you peace. (Numbers 6:24-26 NIV)

6

Tidying Up

A FEW YEARS BACK, a book called *The Life-Changing Magic of Tidying Up* and a spin-off television show brought the wisdom of a petite Japanese lady named Marie Kondo into millions of Western households.

Like a housekeeping evangelist, Marie Kondo came to the rescue of hoarders and overwhelmed clients with tidying tips, and even more importantly, with a philosophical proposal: instead of trying to attain happiness by accumulating more and more stuff, Kondo suggests that too many things—even good things—cannot be enjoyed.

The "Kondo method" is her solution. If a person will commit to the method, Marie promises it will improve their peace and happiness at home.

The method is simple. Marie coaches clients to go through their homes forming piles of belongings. Room by room and category by category they pull everything out and form great stacks. All the shoes. All the papers. All the books. It's a shocking display of accumulation. Once all within a certain category has been amassed, clients must go through one piece at a time—a pair of shoes, a paperback book, etc.— to determine whether it *sparks joy* in their heart.

"Spark joy" is Kondo's catchphrase and her standard of appraisal. It is a perfect way to test the value of something based on what it adds to one's overall quality of life. It has nothing to do with what the item costs, or how impressive it is, or even how brilliantly crafted it might be. It's about whether or not the object resonates with the internal tuning fork of joy deep within the owner's heart.

For example, a certain coat might be trendy, but if it doesn't spark joy, it has to go. Each item that takes up space—chair, picture frame, stack of old magazines—has to earn its place in the limited area of one's home by bringing something essentially *good* to one's life.

SCHEDULE HOARDING

The writer Annie Dillard famously said, "How we spend our days is, of course, how we spend our lives. What we do with this hour, and that one, is what we are doing." If we want to spend our lives connecting deeply with God and people and savoring wonderful experiences, it will come down at last to small choices about how we use our days, hours, even minutes.

Do we use them well? Or have we packed them so full that we hardly enjoy any of it?

You see, our lives have limited space, and when it comes to to-do lists and daily activities, many of us live a bit like hoarders. We pile up commitments and cram appointments into spare rooms. Eventually, our days are completely, appallingly full. We aren't able to savor the sweetness of ordinary moments or soak in the glory of grand occasions because there's so much other stuff in the way.

This happens to me seasonally—with my house and my calendar! I might look at other people's schedules and think, *Who has time for that?* But I have my own stockpiling issues.

It doesn't mean everything I've signed up for is bad. Just *too much*.

When I try to maintain too many calendar commitments—many of them related to my kids—it creates a rushed, joyless schedule for the whole family. I've seen it crowd out the empty spaces that we need to finish a conversation or wind down at the end of the day. The results are shallow, hurried interactions and tired minds and bodies.

Kids are all too often victims of schedule overload. With the best of intentions, we sometimes imagine that the way to nurture a wholesome childhood is to pack it full of things to do—excursions, social visits, tutors, culturally enriching shows and museum tours, sports, music lessons, and on and on. The image of the ideal parent that we carry in our subconscious can sometimes resemble a hotel concierge or a travel agent—a master itinerary planner, transportation coordinator, and guru of memorable experiences.

But this isn't who children actually need us to be.

What kids really need and want from grown-ups is deep connection. Not an impressive, nonstop schedule. (If they seem to crave that, it's because we've cultivated their appetite for it.)

Now, don't misunderstand. I'm not suggesting we should forgo all adventures and learning opportunities. We'll be exploring many such soul-nourishing experiences in this book. But it's hard for kids to be fully present and engaged in each experience when the day is crammed with stimulating activities. And it's hard for *us* to be fully present and engaged with our kids when we are rushing from thing to thing, managing the itinerary. Overbooking kids' schedules with exciting and enriching activities can actually compete with the higher goal of connecting with them.

To know each other deeply, we need less activity, not more. We're so thoroughly soaked in the idea that we need to keep the fun times rolling that this might sound hard to believe, but bonding with kids happens best in simple, unspectacular blocks of time. Sitting and talking, working around the house, eating together at home—simple activities that would never make the travel agent's list are the primary spaces where relationships unfold. One of the greatest things you can offer children is just yourself, fully available.

SLOWING IT DOWN BY TIDYING UP

If we look at Jesus' lifestyle, we can see a healthy way to curate what goes into a day.

Jesus had plenty to do, but he made space in his day to give attention to the people he was with and to nurture constant communion with his heavenly Father. He wasted no time on things—even good things—that weren't for him, weren't his calling. So he was free to experience work, rest, refreshment, and friendship in healthy proportions that sustained his spirit with God's abundant grace.

When Jesus says, "Follow me" he is inviting us to imitate his way of life, including his daily rhythms and the way he organized his time (see, e.g., Luke 9:23). Although practicing the way of Jesus can look like missing out on some things, he doesn't leave us to wonder whether it will all be worth it: "I came that they may have *zoë* and have it abundantly" (John 10:10). *Zoë* is Jesus' word for a whole and holy, vibrant, eternal life. And the primary mark of that life is joy, because it makes time for the greatest gift of all—close communion with God. Nearness to God *sparks joy*.

King David said it this way:

> You show me the path of life.
> > In your presence there is fullness of joy;
> > in your right hand are pleasures for evermore. (Psalm 16:11)

David and Jesus speak from their lived experience. The abundance of a good life does not come from stockpiling experiences and rushing to do more but from savoring each moment as an opportunity to be with God and to act in harmony with his purposes.

If we want the good life Jesus lived and preached, we need to take inventory of all the stuff crowding our calendars and pare way, way down so that the things that help us find joy in God's presence are not shoved on a shelf or buried under a pile of other agenda items. That's where I think Marie Kondo's tidying up method can help. If we adapt Kondo's standard of appraisal, in conversation with the Holy Spirit, we can discern what things in our schedules spark joy and what's just taking up space.

Look back into your memory banks and let the Holy Spirit remind you of what you already know. Activities that stick with us, that really bring us joy, are often simple things. Do you remember savoring any of these childhood activities?

- Trying to swing as high as the clouds and feeling airborne
- Performing homemade plays or dance routines for your family
- Sledding on a crisp winter morning
- Thumbing through family photo albums
- Sitting on the porch or chasing fireflies on a summer night
- Skateboarding around the neighborhood
- Listening to grown-ups laugh and tell family stories
- Looking for ghost crabs with flashlights on the beach at night

Maybe one of these examples sparks a little thrill of childhood joy. In most cases, the things we remember most fondly would never make the tourism guidebook. And we are only alive to the beauty of such moments when our schedules are not packed so tightly. Tidying up is a way to bring our schedule hoarding out of hiding and into the light of God's gaze, to clear space for that which is truly beneficial.

HOW TO PRACTICE TIDYING UP

A family shares a schedule the same way they share a home. Up to a certain age, children don't really have a say over what's on the schedule. They live at the mercy of family routines. So it's up to us— parents and caregivers, teachers and friends—to start by cleaning up our personal calendars. The trick is to pare down the accumulated items on your schedule just as you would clear out a packed closet—let go of what isn't working for you. Your life is valuable real estate, and you don't need to make space for any of these common time-stealers:

- To-dos taken on to keep up appearances or impress someone
- Routines left over from a different stage of life that no longer fit

- Joy impostors—things you do to zone out or get a quick hit of pleasure, which ironically leave you more depleted

- Trends that don't suit you—popular activities that work great for other folks but don't align with your unique calling and life circumstances

Once we have tidied up our personal agendas we can reconsider which kid-centered activities make the cut. Activities need to *earn* their place in our children's valuable minutes, hours, and days. Cramming in too much does not protect the sanctity of their time.

We can seek the Spirit's guidance as to what should make the cut by once again using the "spark joy" question. Pull everything you've hoarded on your family schedule out where you can see it. Use sticky notes or a flip chart, and list *all* the things your kids are doing during their waking hours. We need to see how much we've accumulated, and then assess every item taking up space here.

Does this bring my child joy?

Do they have time for the good, wholesome pleasures of childhood?

When have I seen them alert and engaged?

Who do they love spending time with?

What will bring my child closer to God, the source of all joy?

The answers to these questions can guide us as we let go of things that don't spark joy or that represent too much of a good thing.

Here are a few general rules of thumb for tidying up your family's schedule and some tips for figuring out what stays and what goes:

1. *Leave some blank space.* Kids need unscheduled time. Lulls between activities prevent rush and stress. And blank space gives children of all ages a chance to feel bored. Boredom is the gateway to self-propelled play and creative outpourings like writing, drawing, composing, choreographing, and building. Have you ever seen a playroom with so many toys in it that

there's no floor space left to play? It's the same with our calendars—the more open space in the schedule, the more room your child has to get immersed in something they love doing.

2. *Make a Favorite Things To Do list.* Like Fräulein Maria's famous song, a family list of favorite things can remind us what sparks joy—the extra-special moments as well as the ordinary activities. Try making the list on a car trip or sometime when you're all sitting around together. It might surprise you to learn what your kids put on the list and what they leave off. Ask teens and young adults what they loved to do best as little kids and add those to the list as well. We're never too old to return to some of these favorites!

If you or your kids have trouble populating the list, or if it tilts toward only expensive activities, it might be a sign that the family schedule has been too overloaded for small things to stand out in your memories. Not to worry; this is something you can shift over time by paring down and highlighting sweet, or-dinary times. When commemorating special moments in the family photo album, include not only grand events but im-promptu moments of tenderness and delight. Make a mental note of unspectacular activities and settings that bring out something wonderful in your child—affection, independence, contentment, or creativity. These belong on the Favorite Things To Do list. Revisit the list at different stages of life to see what changes.

3. *Make space in the schedule for things that* **aren't** *fun.* A well-paced day includes favorite activities as well as things we do because they need doing. A lot of times kids today are victims of over-full schedules because parents and grand-parents want to create a magical Disneyland life that soars from one mountaintop experience to another. But responsibility offers kids a different kind of satisfaction. Responsibilities

might not register on the Favorite Things list, but that doesn't mean they have to be completely joyless. Every activity in life can be done *with* God, and there is joy in doing meaningful work and helping others. That's a perspective that can sustain kids as they age up into the responsibilities of adulthood. Plus, when our days aren't so jam-packed, the not-fun things feel less burdensome.

4. ***Give tweens and teens a shot at setting their own schedule.*** Transition your role from curator to coach as a child ages up. Just as we gradually give children more responsibility with helping around the house, it's healthy to involve kids in making decisions about how they spend their time. If we protect their time in early years and teach them how to tidy a schedule as they get older, they will be less likely to fall into schedule-hoarding habits. On a vacation week, or whenever you have a few days where the schedule isn't already set, give your child the freedom to decide how they'll spend their time. Have them map their itinerary on paper so they can visualize it and show it to you for (light) feedback. Teens can have an especially hard time preserving space for sleep, for family connection, and for spiritually nourishing activities. But make this an opportunity for them to learn by experience what was too much. At the end of the time, ask them how it went. What would they change? What worked well, in their opinion? Be affirming of all their good decisions and be honest if you think they need to work on paring down. As always, adapt this practice to your child's unique personality and maturity.

You can also share the tidying up metaphor and this chapter with older children. See if they like the idea. (My daughter did!) Share about your own struggles and triumphs with scheduling, and invite your child to be a partner in the mission to prioritize joy in the family schedule.

Marie Kondo's approach to tidying a house requires equal measures of determination, discernment, and gratitude. When you find something that doesn't lead to life and joy and wholeness, you *need* to let it go, but you can do so without disgust or anger. Perhaps something no longer fits or serves a helpful purpose in your life; you can be thankful for the gifts it offered you in a previous season as you let it go. Perhaps someone gave you an item that you don't have room for; you can decide to let it go without begrudging the other person. Balance and gratitude can mark our calendar-clearing as well.

Dallas Willard famously told one of his students, "You must ruthlessly eliminate hurry from your life." And Paul spoke in even more extreme language: "Put to death" whatever stands between you and the life that is truly life (Colossians 3:5). I appreciate how such wording helps us understand the gravity of the situation. The health of our souls is at stake, and self-indulgence will make us hang on to things we really need to let go of.

But let me offer a word of caution: we must be careful that in pursuing our own soul's growth we don't do harm to those around us—children, neighbors, relatives, friends—by being hasty or harsh. Our schedules are intricately woven together with our children's lives. Deciding what to let go of and what to preserve is slow, discerning, almost surgical work. We can't just ax everything that makes us tired or adds complexity to our daily routine. If you've spent twenty-four hours tending to a child with a stomach bug—going to the doctor, sitting up through the night, changing sheets, serving soup and jello—your day has been full and exhausting. But this is not schedule hoarding. This is pouring yourself out in love, and it produces a deep joy centered in the other person's well-being. Savage determination to reach a minimalist schedule or a shallow take on the "spark joy" question could lead us to resent some of life's most important opportunities to connect, love, and serve.

We need a gentle touch as we clean up our schedules. That's why we must seek God's perspective to guide our calendar-clearing. Living in alignment with the kingdom of God reorients us to true sources of joy—like the joy of caring for your sick child.

So bring your agenda items before the Lord.

If something isn't for you, release it gently, with gratitude.

Let the Spirit guide you in the path of life.

7

Speed Checks

I HAVE A FRIEND WHO SPENT fifty-something years as a speed demon behind the wheel. He loved the sensation of flying down the highway. And he had business engagements that made going eighty miles per hour on the New Jersey Turnpike a lucrative practice. A few years back he felt moved to review this habit with the Lord, and he decided to take on a spiritual discipline of driving ten miles under the speed limit.

He's retired.

When he told me about his new discipline and how God had been using it to cultivate his attention and his inward sense of calm, my first thought ran something like this: *Well, good for you! Maybe someday I'll have the luxury of retirement and an empty nest. And then, sure, I'll go forty in a fifty zone. For now, I'm going to keep pushing sixty so we get to school on time.*

My second thought was something like this (and I'm embarrassed to confess it): *Your spiritual discipline might be good for you, but it sounds terrible for everyone else. What about the folks behind you who genuinely need to get to the doctor or the meeting? You can't force other people to slow down with you!*

But the reason his story really bothered me is that it convicted me. I'm always in a hurry. I overpack the schedule and leave no margin for delays. You better believe I'm counting on going over the speed limit to make up for leaving five minutes behind schedule. Slowpokes, like my disciplined friend, are the saboteurs of my strategy.

Haste is a habit that not only marks my car travel but can spill over into how I go through my day's activities: Make the dinner as fast as possible. Knock out the grocery shopping in between two other tasks and scrimp on transition times. Schedule a work meeting to take one hour when it really needs two.

For years, I made quickness a virtue because I am a good hurrier. And my rush-to-squeeze-in-more approach has served me well enough.

But then came parenthood.

Parenthood is like pulling off the highway still going seventy and getting behind a bicycle. It's a *dramatic* pace adjustment to accommodate a little slowpoke human. And it feels all the more uncomfortable for those of us who regularly push the speed limit of daily living.

TRYING TO HURRY KIDS ALONG

If you try to impose the robust itinerary and agile pace of adulthood on little ones, you will be sorely frustrated. Kids don't hurry very well. The more you need them to hurry up—just a little, just this once, *pretty please!*—the more slowly they are likely to go.

To let children grow up, you have to let them start trying to do things themselves. They need unhurried time to practice walking, to learn to tie a shoe, to draw the letter *E*, to read a sentence one halting word at a time.

A mind-boggling biological discovery that helps illustrate the point is the way mammal milk production works. The foremilk at the start of a feeding is relatively watery. But the hindmilk that comes at the end of the feeding is more nutrient rich and has a higher fat content. If you rush a nursing session, the baby will get only the skim stuff. Babies need an entire feeding, unrushed and uninterrupted, to get the nutrients that help them feel full, sleep better, and continue the wondrous development of brain and body.

And it isn't just babies who shouldn't be rushed.

My sister Catherine, the youngest of us three Pate kids, remembers an incident from our family's big trip to Italy when she was thirteen. The trip was a celebration of several milestones: I had graduated from college, my brother had graduated from high school, and Catherine had finished middle school. We were only in Italy for two weeks, so we were trying to squeeze in as much as we could. ("Squeezing in as much as you can" being the obvious and normal thing to do.) As a young teen in the middle of a growth spurt, my little sister didn't have the same stamina as the rest of us or as much interest in the historical sites. She recalls standing in the Sistine Chapel and asking our dad, "How much longer do we have to stay here?"

Bless her heart! Here we were standing beneath Michelangelo's masterpiece—a treasured landmark and one of the world's most awe-inspiring depictions of God and humanity—and Catherine just wanted to be done with it. The fast-moving itinerary had maxed out her capacity for awe. The Sistine Chapel became just one more site on the whirlwind tour.

"I know I should have appreciated it more," Catherine apologized when she told me this story. But the truth is, any child that age would have had a similar response. Some of this is just the unavoidable toll of international travel. But if we could do it over again, I think our whole family would want to adjust the pace to better accommodate the youngest one in our midst.

The significance isn't lost on me that this episode happened in a magnificent physical space designed to draw people near to the Lord in prayer and worship. When children are rushed, it isn't only their human interactions that are incapacitated. None of us—young or old—can be present to God without the chance to fully arrive, to adjust our bodies and brains to our surroundings, to "be still, and know" that God is near (Psalm 46:10). You can see it in Bible stories, and you can probably recognize it in your own life: People are most likely to encounter God at moments in their lives where everything has slowed way down.

That's why hurry is a form of violence to a child's thriving. Heaven and earth are full of God's glory (see Isaiah 6:3), but if we hurry kids along, they won't have the capacity to take it in. It pains me to say it, because on the ledger of my conscience there is a tally of my own offenses—all the times I've barked orders, yelled "hurry up!" and all but dragged my family to match my own pace. God, forgive me! God, deliver me from this habit!

If you feel this way too, take heart. Even with my bad track record and habit of rushing, there have been some small victories and steps forward (intermingled with a few steps back) as I have cooperated with God's invitations to reset the pace.

SLOWING IT DOWN WITH SPEED CHECKS

We may not perceive what the right speed is when we are accustomed to going so fast. *Psychology Today* describes a phenomenon that we have probably all experienced at some point:

> Drive for an hour at 65 mph on an interstate alongside other vehicles moving at similar speeds. Then take an exit ramp onto a quiet street with no other visible vehicles traveling at your pace. You slow down; however, with nothing to indicate otherwise, you are likely traveling far faster than the local speed limit. **The mind has to readjust to take in a new reality of motion**.

The pace of modern life is interstate-speed. Rapid transit, digital connections, and hustle culture have set a brisk and demanding pace. People go, go, go. They can't stop or stay to visit. They look for the fast lane. Caught up in the press of these cultural habits, I begin to match that pace and let those values and expectations dictate my speed.

In sharp contrast, the pace of my soul's thriving is like the quiet street off the exit ramp. It's a slower way of life where I can live tuned into God, wide-awake to beauty, community, and family, and able to savor life. How does one adjust to that "new reality of motion"?

Speed checks can help.

You know, the little roadside scanners that flash your miles per hour and say *SLOW DOWN* when you're going over the limit? When it comes to our pace of life, speed checks are God's signals—through our bodies and emotions, and through the feedback of other people and the world around us—that let us know we're going too fast for soul-nourishing connections.

God isn't a cosmic policeman looking to bust us. He uses spiritual speed checks to alert us that we are being reckless with our souls or with our children's souls. He wants to help us get our bearings and adjust to a pace where we can take in the reality of his presence with awe and savor the life he has given us.

Being married to William has been a nineteen-years-and-counting speed check. My husband is never in a rush. Which is great . . . unless I'm in a hurry. Running late does not affect William's mood or his miles per hour. He'll stop to chat with the neighbor even if we are on our way to a wedding—even if he is the one officiating the wedding! Sometimes I appreciate this trait. However, I wouldn't feel good about publishing this book without confessing that mostly it irritates me to death. I bet nine out of ten arguments in our marriage have been related in some way or another to schedule and speed. The irritation that I feel when William is moving slowly can serve as a spiritual speed check if I notice the sensation and heed it as a warning, take some deep breaths, and readjust my pace.

I can sympathize with the disciples' frustration when their buddy Jesus just couldn't stick to the schedule they had in mind. On one road trip to Galilee, Jesus stopped by a well, struck up a conversation with a Samaritan woman, and ended up staying several days in her village (John 4:1-33). Another time, when Mary and Martha sent word that their brother Lazarus was very sick, Jesus puzzled everyone by waiting two days to go to them (John 11). Jesus was a living rebuke to the hurry of those around him.

Even as a child, Jesus didn't comply with the expected flow of traffic. On a trip to Jerusalem with his family, the travel party left to return to Nazareth assuming that Jesus was in their midst. But he stayed back. His parents were understandably frantic, and they scolded him when they found him. "His mother said to him, 'Child, why have you treated us like this? Your father and I have been anxiously looking for you.' He said to them, 'Why were you searching for me? Did you not know that I must be in my Father's house?'" (Luke 2:48-49). The Greek text lacks the word *house*. Instead, it is identical to Jesus' statement later in his life: "I am in my Father" (John 14:20). He was intent on communicating his union with the Father, and perhaps this childhood statement is an early teaching on that reality. His sense of timing, even as a child, revolved around preserving that relationship.

Mary and Joseph were perplexed by their son's answer. "They did not understand this spiritual doctrine he spoke about himself" (Luke 2:50, my translation). It's complicated to our ears too. Jesus' unity with the Father is unique and miraculous. And yet even he had to resist being swept along with the current of human movement in order to maintain that union.

If this is true of the incarnate Son, how much more must we guard against losing touch with our heavenly Father in the frantic rush of modern living!

HOW TO PRACTICE SPEED CHECKS

Children seem to have an internal sense of right and wrong about pacing. Do you have a memory of being rushed as a kid? What did it feel like in your body and in your emotions? Those little alarm bells were God-given speed checks, teaching you to crave a healthier pace. So pay attention to your child's emotions and behaviors. If your child is being rushed, here are some *SLOW DOWN* signals you might see:

- **Meltdowns, trouble focusing, exhaustion, and anxiety.**
  Many things can cause these symptoms, but it's wise to rule out pacing first. Is there enough space between activities for your child to mentally prepare for the next thing? Is the speed of

the conversation, school assignment, or itinerary too fast for them? Dig into the *why* behind behaviors before you discipline or medicate to see if the problem is pace of life. Gentleness is good medicine.

- ■ ***Underdeveloped independence.*** Letting kids do things themselves can be painstakingly slow. If you try to rush them by saying, "Come on, come on . . . can't you go a little faster?" or "Let me just do that for you," it might save you time in the short term, but it's a poor tradeoff for the long-term goals of self-sufficiency and helpfulness.

- ■ ***Shame and crushed enthusiasm.*** Criticizing kids' pace sends the message that they aren't good enough. Things like learning a new skill or trying to communicate can become humiliating for kids if someone pushes them to go faster than they are able. Some kids are more self-critical by nature, but if you notice a dip in your child's enthusiasm or confidence, check to see if it indicates speed-related pressure.

- ■ ***Shallowness.*** Are your children kind and considerate? Are they sensitive to things that are tender, sad, or stunningly beautiful? Do they discuss their feelings and ideas? If their interests and relationships are very superficial, they might be victims of life in the fast lane.

If any signals indicate that you or your kids need to slow down, experiment with these ways to adjust to a soul-nourishing pace:

1. ***Walk slower.*** On errands, at the zoo, wherever you go. Don't drag children along. They have little legs! Even older kids with growing limbs might need to walk more slowly than you would prefer. Allowing children to move at their own pace isn't only good for them, it develops patience and love in adult caregivers.

2. ***Right-size the importance of punctuality.*** I used to get a little knot in my stomach on the way to gymnastics as a kid because

our coach would berate us for being late. This anxiety about promptness still lingers with me today. The solution isn't to be lazy or disrespectful about arrival times, but to keep a big-picture perspective. Making a flight on time is a big deal, but no one is going to die if you get to soccer practice ten minutes late. I wish I had done better showing my kids by my own attitude that the schedule serves us; we don't serve the schedule.

3. *Extend transition times.* A buffer zone between activities is good for adults, but especially important for kids because their brains take a little longer to switch from one direction of focus to the next. Even teens need transition time; they are easily depleted because *physically* they can keep up with adults but sometimes need longer to arrive mentally and emotionally. So instead of speeding from one thing to the next, pad the schedule with ample time to switch gears. And give kids the courtesy of advance notice. "We'll be leaving in about fifteen minutes, and I'll tell you when we have about five minutes left."

4. *Don't rush kids out of play.* Many crucial ingredients in a child's spiritual and mental development are found at the end of long and uninterrupted play and discovery. If you can recall times as a child when you were allowed to take as long as you liked, I bet those were times when you experienced a sense of peace, maybe even an indescribable awareness that God was with you, or a deep sense of awe for his handiwork. Kids need unhurried time to awaken to these gifts. In truth, we never grow out of this.

5. *Be a pace setter.* If you happen to be in the privileged position of setting standards—as a leader of a church, a team, a children's activity, or a business—remember that you can bless others by making arrival times more flexible. Create a gracious pace. Be the one person in someone's life who lets them off the hook. Don't be the source of hurry.

Adjusting to the pace of God's reality takes some courage. We might annoy people who are still in a rush. But the speedy people aren't good pace setters. We have to keep our sights set on what is truly good for us and especially for young people. We might not be able to change unrealistic expectations around us in the world, but as far as it is up to us, we can relax into the rhythms that protect our children's souls.

8

Singletasking

A Palace in Time

Tidying Up

Speed Checks

Singletasking

WHEN MY SON WAS IN SECOND GRADE, he brought home this Mother's Day acrostic poem:

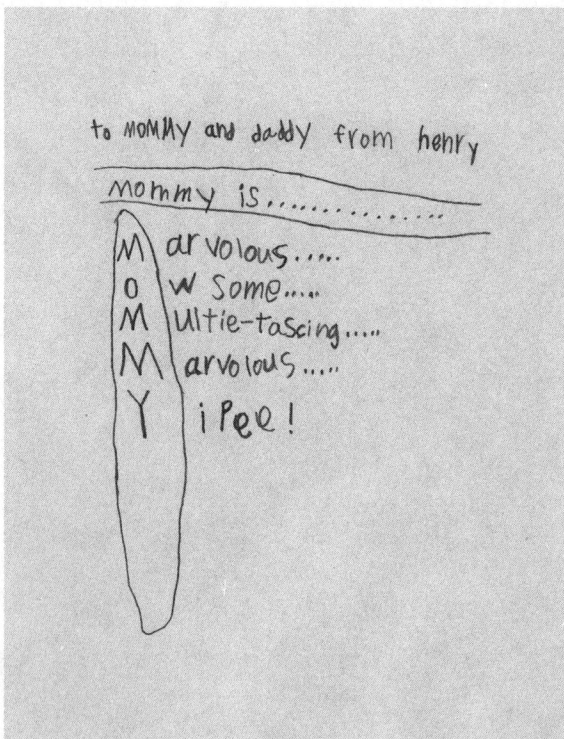

> to MOMMY and daddy from henry
>
> mommy is..............
>
> M arvolous.....
> O w some.....
> M ultie-tascing.....
> M arvolous.....
> Y iPee !

As honored as I was by this "owsome" tribute, I was gutted by the appearance of *multitasking*–phonetically rendered in eight-year-old print. Of all the affirmations Henry could have listed (and that he thought I would be pleased to hear about myself), this was a top adjective! It isn't exactly a warm and fuzzy attribute. If you had to choose whether your child saw you as a generous shoulder to cry on or a boss at getting stuff done, which would you choose?

Henry's gift raised a red flag. Somehow I had sent him the unspoken message that juggling many things at once is normal, even heroic, and that multitasking is a healthy way to manage work . . . and maybe people.

I'm not saying multitasking is always bad. There is great value in being able to attend to several things at once when the situation demands it. But habitual multitasking can be problematic. *Always* doing several things at once means you have too much going on or just prefer spreading your attention in a lot of directions at once.

I've always been a little too fond of multitasking. I love to move quickly, efficiently. To collect accomplishments like pearls strung on a necklace of self-satisfaction. Knocking out several agenda items at once gives me a rush, like time is my opponent and I've just scored the winning shot. But I've come to recognize that this task-oriented mindset can be crushing to those around me.

The satisfaction, even pride, that I feel when concurrently dealing with people and tasks is at odds with the way of Jesus. People don't want to be "dealt with." They want to be loved. And as Dallas Willard says, "The first act of love is always the giving of attention."

OUR SIMULTANEOUS WORLD

The quintessential multitasker from the pages of Scripture is Martha of Bethany, the sister of Mary. When Jesus came to visit these sisters who were his close friends, they reacted very differently to his visit. Martha was deacon-ing hard—you know, serving, doing ministry work, all good stuff (see Luke 10:40). But rather than being available to her friend Jesus, she was distracted by all the preparations that had to be made. (*Had to* . . . in her opinion.) And she was bitter that her sister wasn't helping.

Where was Mary? Well, Mary had seated herself at Jesus' feet to listen, in the posture of a disciple. Her attention to what Jesus was saying and doing wasn't fragmented by extraneous goals. When Martha complained to Jesus about Mary, he answered her, "Martha, Martha, you are worried and distracted by many things, but few things are needed—indeed only one. Mary has chosen the better part, which will not be taken away from her" (Luke 10:41-42).

Do you ever feel distracted from the people around you or from the presence of Christ because you are "worried and distracted by many things"? That's the problem with multitasking. We can't give our attention to any one thing well when we give it to many things at once. It is frustrating to even attempt to be available to Jesus or to any of our dear ones while simultaneously hosting an army of duties and concerns. Of course some of this is unavoidable—show me the parent who doesn't have to call out spelling words while simultaneously unloading the dishwasher! But much of it is self-induced.

In our achievement-oriented culture, multitasking is often a strategy for squeezing more into our schedules than what is good for our souls. I know that we're all good Christian people and well-meaning parents, but we can be guilty of wanting to do God's will *and* check off our own goals, too. (I know I'm guilty!)

This life strategy absolutely impacts our kids. We want them to have *deep* connections with God and others and to engage *deeply* in wholesome activities that nourish their minds, bodies, and spirits. But we also want them to do all the things and keep up with the circus of activity. We shouldn't be surprised, then, if they are incurious and shallow in their interactions with other people and God. A river with a set volume of water can either flow in a deep, narrow channel, or in a broad shallow bed. Human powers of attention are the same.

Attention is especially susceptible to being spread too thin in young people. The human brain is still developing well into the twenties, and the last part to finish developing is the frontal cortex that controls a person's ability to prioritize and manage tasks and ignore distractions. In today's world, kids are expected to move faster and juggle more than they should (developmentally speaking) in order to keep up with us and not upset our spinning plates.

To a certain degree, children need to practice managing multiple demands on their attention so that they can learn to prioritize. But executive functioning develops *slowly*. Harvard's Center on the Developing Child warns that if kids experience certain forms of stress, like the pressure to manage too much too quickly, "their skill development can be seriously delayed or impaired." Ironically, trying to rush kids into simultaneous task execution makes them shut down. They move even slower and have a harder time finishing things.

Rarely do kids choose multitasking. It is usually thrust on them by environments that draw their focus in too many directions and by family habits that interrupt immersive activities or lay a burden of accomplishing too much on a young person. When hurry and hustle are at the root of our multitasking, all of us feel more stressed and less connected.

SLOWING IT DOWN WITH *SINGLETASKING*

A small step we can take toward nurturing inward calm and outward love for others is *singletasking*–choosing to do just one thing, and to do it with our whole attention.

Singletasking is a powerful discipline to put our habits and priorities in check. Remember that Martha was distracted by all the preparations that had to be made, but according to Jesus, those preparations weren't actually needed. So who had decided they had to be made? Martha. Jesus didn't ask her to multitask. She did, for her own reasons or to keep up with the customs of her time and place.

And we do this too–get it in our heads that so much needs doing beyond the actual call of duty. Jesus' words can be our checkpoint when we get this way: "Few things are needed–indeed only one" (Luke 10:42).

I have to slow down enough before plunging into a flurry of activity each day to make a mental list (actually, I write mine down) of all that I think needs doing, and then invite Jesus to bring clarity so that I can sift and simplify. For each item on my list, I can ask: Why did I put it there? Is it really *mine* to do? And if it is mine to do, how can I go about it without worry and distraction? Whenever I choose to pare my list down to just a few things and take them one at a time, it is a life-giving, love-enhancing movement.

And this holds true for children, too. Children will feel better and have more capacity to respond lovingly when they aren't multitasking. Singletasking is an important counterbalance to the habit of rushing young people into task-juggling. It's a way to give them the time and support they need to develop those executive processing and functioning skills without adding unnecessary pressure and frustration. Most importantly, helping kids singletask gives them the chance to give attention—the "first act of love"—to the people around them and to God.

Maybe you can recall someone who gave you the gift of their undivided attention when you were young. Or perhaps you can remember times when you were able to be completely immersed in an activity because you didn't have other tasks to juggle. I remember whittling with my granddad. We sat side by side as he showed me how to draw a shape on a piece of wood and use a carving knife to shape the block into a figure. His unhurried presence and gentle guidance were the embodiment of love. That deep connection would have been lost if other tasks had been added to the schedule. Such experiences in our growing-up years are a gift, and it's worth taking a moment of gratitude for the people who made them possible.

HOW TO PRACTICE SINGLETASKING

To help our children experience the freedom and depth of singletasking, we can draw on the wisdom of our childhood experiences and Jesus' perennially helpful reminder that "few things are needed."

Children are naturally more like Mary. They are ready to let the chores wait and listen deeply to a friend's story. They are ready to get lost in play or discovery—giving it their undivided attention. They don't share the adult fear that doing just one thing is not enough. But kids absorb the values about time that we project. I have to admit that mostly I've tried to teach my children *how to* multitask rather than *how not to.*

"Keep putting those shoes on while you talk to me, son."

"You'll have to finish that homework on the ride to school!"

I'm haunted by Jesus' words to Martha regarding her complaint about Mary: "Mary has chosen the better part, *which will not be taken away from her*" (Luke 10:42, emphasis mine). When kids are moving more slowly than we would like because they are deeply engaged in a soul-nourishing connection or activity, they're actually doing what is best. And we shouldn't take that away from them. Not everything qualifies, of course. The principle of not interrupting kids' immersive experiences only holds when the experience itself is valuable. But don't underestimate the value of just playing.

Pressuring my kids to multitask teaches them to value the volume and speed of accomplishments over the ability to engage deeply and calmly in an activity. It may even teach them to value to-dos more highly than people. I cringe when I think how many times I've drawn them away from what Jesus says is best by my own task-oriented outlook and by hurrying them in multiple directions. Those are the low points.

The high points, looking back, are small victories. But they remind me that a better way is possible, and they signal what's working well. Here are some of our family's singletasking victories and areas where we're currently working on making progress.

1. *Make eye contact.* Gently and gradually, we are helping our
   kids to engage in conversation with better attention. When the
   kids were small, I would often squat down to their eye level so

that they could engage with me face-to-face. Now that they are older, I might ask them to pause what they are doing so we can discuss something—put down the book or the basketball and look at my face while we talk. This helps gather all the powers of attention to a single point of concentration and connection, a skill that translates well into a child's life with God. A note on electronic devices: Not giving our kids personal devices has been one of the easiest and most effective ways we have found to nurture their immersive experiences and deep connections with people.

2. ***Sit down for family dinner.*** Before we had kids, we sometimes ate supper on the sofa while we caught an episode of something. But once Charlotte was born, we realized that wasn't how we wanted dinner to be in our family. So we made the switch to eating at the table. We've kept up a sit-down dinner for the past fifteen years now. It isn't any major victory to singletask mealtimes, but I know that if we didn't make the effort, it would be just one more part of our day where we would be trying to do five things at once. And we would be less connected with each other because of it. If you want to establish the habit of a family meal, here's how to get started: Put activities, work, and devices on pause. Ask questions, share about your day, and savor the food and the company. That stage between a high chair and about second grade can be excruciating as children may attempt to pop up from their seats a hundred times per meal. Older kids might be tempted to reach for other activities too. But hang in there! Meals can become a sacred space for connection if you keep other tasks on hold.

3. ***Play together with abandon.*** Sometimes grown-ups need to get out of the way so kids can enter a deep, soul-nourishing flow of imaginative play. But in my experience, finding regular opportunities to play along with my kids has strengthened our

relationship and enhanced (not weakened) their ability to play creatively and contentedly on their own. When I struggle to play along, it's usually because I'm multitasking. My husband is a natural singletasker and therefore a great playmate for our kids. Here is his suggestion for how to fully enter the flow of play: Stop everything for a while (an hour, or even two). Set aside your other to-dos. And go ahead and set aside any attempt to manage the play time. Let your child be in charge of the activity or the hang-out time. Don't try to accomplish educational goals or guide the time toward a desired outcome or conversation topic. Just give your child your eyes and ears and follow their lead. As best you can, enter the pretend world or creative enterprise your child has dreamed up and give it your all.

4. ***Create checklists.*** Making a checklist helps a child visualize and focus on one task at a time rather than conceptually juggling everything at once. With preschoolers, create a very short list of three or four things and use pictures rather than words. "First we're going to go visit Nana. Then we are going to the grocery store. After that, we are going to play in the park." The point isn't measuring accomplishments; it teaches kids to order their functioning and to think in steps. Elementary-age kids can check off a list you make for them and learn to make their own with your help. Over time decrease your support so that they're doing their own prioritizing. Recently when I had a major traffic jam of projects at work, my supervisor met with me to catalog, sort, and narrow down the deluge of to-dos. It was such a gift to be heard, to be asked clarifying questions, to have his sympathy for my heavy load and to hear his perspective on what I could push off until later. Getting the things out of our heads and onto the page is a powerful reality check that can reveal when we're simply trying to do too much. One of the best things you can do for your stressed-out teen or young adult child is to ask them to

tell you what all they have going on. Listen well, and offer to take down a list. Your attention communicates your care, and the checklist shrinks an avalanche of tasks down to steps that they can handle one at a time.

Savoring time with one another and engaging deeply and calmly in the present moment requires a schedule that is slower not only at the macro-level, but also spacious and uncrowded at any given instant. We can practice and teach our children to practice stepping back periodically to prayerfully consider the question: *What is actually needed at this moment? Are any of the tasks I'm still holding on to unnecessary?* If God prompts us to multitask in order to love someone well, then we should do it. But if it is driven by some other pressure or personal agenda, then it isn't helpful. The way of Jesus always illuminates the greatest task: love. And to do that, usually fewer things are needed than we think.

PART 3

Slow Media

EVERY DAY, SIGHTS AND SOUNDS fly at me from the moment I crack open the cocoon of my personal space.

Thirty-seven new messages. 2,552 archived emails, some of which I still need to read. Who-knows-how-many pings and alerts and fresh posts are waiting to dazzle me on any of the apps I might open.

This is how we live now—surrounded by communication, information, and entertainment that is hyper-speed and intrusive. I don't know about you, but my senses are weary.

The other day at a gas station, the small panel at the pump came to life and started yelling at me about a new movie at the box office. I got back in the car and slammed the door. Is there nowhere we can go without being pumped full of noise?

No matter who I ask, "What holds kids back from savoring childhood?" I can feel frustration boiling beneath the surface about the way that media forces its way in—especially the way that it intrudes on children's eyes and ears.

It's not that communication, information, and entertainment are new to the world. There have always been ways to overindulge in any of these. But never before has media been so high-speed, portable, and pervasive. Even ten years ago the way we accessed media was different. Today's digital environment is unprecedented. There literally is no comparison in history, which makes it tricky to form a wise response. Where is the Bible playbook for this?

The way forward may not be spelled out explicitly in Scripture or mapped out by our Christian brothers and sisters in previous generations, but the sturdy promise throughout all the ages is this: God does not hide from us or scoff at our predicaments. The Shepherd loves us. He will not abandon us. In fact, he already knows a way to navigate us through this mess. So as we pray for God to show us how to respond to fast media, we can be on the lookout for his cues. What parts of Jesus' life illuminate the way? What lessons from the past can signpost the path to a good life, even in the midst of this great fog?

I have been spending time with the story of God meeting with Moses in the burning bush.

> Moses was keeping the flock of his father-in-law Jethro, the priest of Midian; he led his flock beyond the wilderness, and came to Mount Horeb, the mountain of God. There the angel of the Lord appeared to him in a flame of fire out of a bush; he looked, and the bush was blazing, yet it was not consumed. Then Moses said, "I must turn aside and look at this great sight and see why the bush is not burned up." When the Lord saw that he had turned aside to see, God called to him out of the bush, "Moses, Moses!" And he said, "Here I am." (Exodus 3:1-4)

What do you think Moses was doing—or not doing—when he noticed that strange, fiery spot on the landscape? What habit of observation helped him to look closer and see that it was ablaze with an unusual kind of fire—something that burned without consuming the plant? And what prompted him to go over and investigate?

The whole curious display might have gone unnoticed had Moses been preoccupied! He was occupied with shepherding, sure. But he was fully present in the place and work before him, and he had eyes to see and ears to hear. His attention was free. His mind was open and available. His curiosity was God-sharpened and God-directed.

This is the kind of freedom to be present and attentive that we want for our children and for ourselves. In this section of *Savoring Childhood*, we will explore some ways we can release our children from fast media's hold. When we think of our children's safety, we naturally think of physical dangers they might face. But one of the best ways we can help our kids have a safe, healthy childhood is to free them from assaults on their attention. Give them back their eyes and ears.

It is up to us, as partners with God in shepherding his young lambs, to push back the onrush of media. I'm certainly not suggesting businesses and bad actors aren't at fault—they are. I'm saying that we can't wait around for advertisers and entertainers and political campaigns to look out for our children's best interests. We are responsible.

All of us—children and adults—have been exposed to stimulating media to the point that it feels normal. We might even be addicted to it. When we dial back our intake, the depth of our dependency comes to light, and we might experience symptoms of withdrawal.

I say lean into it.

Discomfort is a sign that your appetite is roaring back to life, weaned off the junk that was keeping the good yearnings deep inside of you anesthetized. So whether you are frustrated, fed up, antsy, irritated, or in despair, let those yearnings drive you toward the One who wants to be found.

We are made for connection with God. Our kids are too. And God is right here, as close as the air we breathe! He will not force his way into our awareness. Most of life's beautiful and important things are subtle that way; if our eyes and ears are already overwhelmed, we'll miss them. The stream of content and noise will rush on, but God can show us how to liberate our powers of perception from bondage to it. In the chapters that follow I will share several ways our family has been able to slow down our intake, turn down the volume, and regularly exit the stream.

"When you search for me, you will find me; if you seek me with all your heart," says the Lord (Jeremiah 29:13). If we do our part to reach out with our minds and our senses, we will find the Holy One, and we will be able to live with our eyes and ears available to one another. Our Good Shepherd wants to lead us to a more peaceful stream of communication, information, and content that doesn't compete with savoring childhood.

9

Offloading

LET ME DESCRIBE A SCENE FOR YOU from *The Crown* (a TV drama about the British royal family).

It's shortly after Princess Diana's death, and her older son, William, has just returned to boarding school.

The teenager walks into his dorm room and drops his bookbag on the floor. Another figure enters the room behind him. It's the dormitory housemaster who tells William that there are two deliveries for him. One, a wooden box marked *POST*, contains what the housemaster says are condolences from more than six hundred boys at the school. "That's so kind," William says, trying to take in the overwhelming display of affection.

The second delivery is a large canvas bag full of letters and fan mail from all over the world—"mostly from young ladies," the housemaster says. Desperately missing his mum, William sits down to read some of the post. The letters from schoolmates are personal, tender. Their effect on William is clearly heartwarming.

Then, dutifully, William begins to read the mail from strangers. The girls send their condolences. Their photographs. Their adoring compliments. "Willsmania" is what the newspapers called it—the international obsession over the young British prince among starstruck teenage girls.

A few days later, two more bags of fan mail cramp the small space between the desk and the bed in William's room.

The housemaster checks in on his young charge and finds him sitting on the edge of his bed staring at the bags, shoulders hunched— as if the weight of the letters is more than he can bear. Thankfully, the housemaster senses the burden. He can see that the sheer magnitude of the correspondence is too much for a child. For anyone.

"Would you ... like me to dispose of them?" he asks, nodding toward the mailbags.

Clearly relieved by this offer, William thanks him, and the man carries the burden out of the room and out of the boy's life.

This fictionalized scene gripped my attention. It was unsettling and oddly familiar. Piles of mail. A teenager's anxiety as communications accumulate relentlessly, far beyond what he can handle. It sounds a lot like the too-fast stream of emails, pings, texts, alerts, DMs, snaps, and so forth that kids today shoulder on a daily basis. The average fourteen-year-old with a smart phone receives 192 alerts per day— enough to easily fill a mailbag. Very little of the content that gets transmitted digitally is personal or valuable, but it quickly accumulates into an unmanageable bulk of written and visual messages.

RIPTIDE

Childhood communication—and adult communication, for that matter—hasn't always been so burdensome. In the evolution of communication technology, every increase in transmission speed has been heralded as a win for humankind. Wi-Fi today connects at a rate a hundred times faster than earlier broadband internet connections. And since the release of smartphones put Wi-Fi in our pockets, back-and-forth messaging can be both instant and constant. Supposedly, this improves our quality of life.

Does it? Or does it feel more like we are drowning?

Communications fly at us constantly throughout the day. A single thought, a random joke, a picture. Instead of saving our thoughts for face-to-face communication, we fire off digital messages. The ease and speed of these interactions mean we rarely sift their importance or weigh their urgency. The effect is overwhelming. Writer Lara d'Entremont describes the feeling: "I participated in a group chat with several women I had connected with online (never in person), and my phone buzzed literally hundreds of times in the course of a day.... Whenever I opened the app twenty-four hours later, 200–999 unread messages awaited me. Many of the messages were simply funny stories and memes.... I didn't have the capacity for it all. I deleted the app and left the chat."

The exact number of messages each day differs from person to person, depending on access to (or personal adoption of) online messaging tools. But to a certain extent, being human in our digital age means bearing a load of communication exponentially heavier and faster-paced than any previous generation could have imagined. To participate in most organized activities and communities, you have to get an app, subscribe to the newsletter, or join a group text.

Attempting to go against that current by leaving the chat or ignoring the texts can feel like fighting a cultural riptide. If adults struggle to keep up with all of this, just imagine how our children feel. No wonder they are depressed and anxious! I think most of us sense the burden. We want things to change. We just need a vision of how to set kids free.

SLOWING IT DOWN BY OFFLOADING

I want to return to the heroic housemaster from *The Crown*—the man who removes the mailbags from Prince William's life and sets him free. His simple act of spiritual rescue stuck with me long after I'd watched the show as a clue for how to love children well in an age of excessive communication.

We can be this man!

If we really care about young people and about our own sanity and capacity, let's cut free. Let's offload the digital mail that weighs kids down and steals their joy—as much of it as we possibly can.

Of course there will be some correspondence that we need to keep up. But most of the messages that crowd our lives and our children's lives these days aren't important, aren't even personal. They're riddled with unnecessary announcements from advertisers or random bits of chatter and self-promotion from people we barely know. Even many of the interchanges with folks we know and love could just as well be saved for face-to-face interaction.

Offloading doesn't have to look like reverting to the Dark Ages. Most of us grew up before e-*anything* existed. We still communicated, and we still used technology. But the tools we had were limited in ways that didn't bury us in messages beyond what a person can handle. When you were a kid, how did you keep in touch with friends? How were assignments and school messages transmitted? Do you remember how it felt to be able to walk away from communication media—actually leave it physically behind for periods of time?

I'm not suggesting we try to recreate the past, but we can take small steps back toward the communication habits of our own childhoods by offloading *some* of the apps and gadgets that keep us swimming in messages these days. Delete apps, clear inboxes, leave group chats, use analog forms of communication. Drastically simplified delivery systems prevent the bulk of digital transmissions from reaching our kids.

I believe the solution is that simple. And at the same time, I realize that fast communication has become so intertwined with our lives that setting children free from it feels impossible—even laughable. But we can't assume that things are too far gone for Jesus to help us turn them around. Consider the Bible story where Jesus was asked to help a twelve-year-old girl who was very sick and close to death. While Jesus was on the way to her house, a message arrived saying it was too late. The girl had succumbed to her illness. Jesus proceeded anyway and reassured the crowd that he could help the girl. But blinded by their own assumptions about what was possible, "they laughed at him"

(Mark 5:40). Imagine their surprise when the girl emerged, alive and restored by Jesus.

The task ahead of us may feel insurmountable, but the Miracle Worker is with us, and it is his love, wisdom, and guidance that will empower us to set kids free.

HOW TO PRACTICE OFFLOADING

Let's dig into the *how*. We've already noted that we need to preserve some modes of communicating, but which ones can we cut loose? What does it look like in a real family, living in the real world, to offload in a way that is life-giving and sustainable? Here are some practices that have worked for our kids and have helped William (my husband, not the prince) and me to offload our own burdensome communications.

1. ***Encourage relatives and friends to actually call*** and use their voice on the phone instead of texting. The pace of conversation is slower, and the messages don't accumulate in the burdensome way that digital transmissions do. In texts and emails, say, "Let's finish talking about this when we see each other next." Whenever you can, catch up in person. Eliminating non-urgent back-and-forths lessens the bulk of your child's mailbag. Plus, if you text throughout the day with your teenager, you might not have much to say to each other when you get together in person. We've found it enriches our time together as a family if we *aren't* sharing updates constantly throughout the day.

2. ***Set boundaries for older kids with cell phones.*** First of all, cell phones aren't right for every child, because each kid is different. If having a phone adds to your child's anxiety and distraction or they can't abide by healthy boundaries, set them free and just get rid of it. They won't think it's freedom, but your job is to protect them, not to appease them. If your child is responsible

enough to observe your boundaries, here are some of the rules we've used with Charlotte to guard against an onslaught of notifications:

- One messaging platform is enough (e.g., iMessage).

- We have set Charlotte's phone to be dormant between 10 p.m. and 7 a.m. Restricted hours guard the sanctity of sleep.

- Remind kids that they don't have to answer texts and calls right away. Just slowing down the back and forth drastically reduces the bulk of transmissions.

- No social media. It's not just the negative and depressing content or exposure to predators and marketers that makes these platforms dangerous. It's also the inhumane number of messages that a vast social network dumps on our kids. Going without social media is challenging for kids. They will be less visible and less looped in on the drama and chatter of their peers. But it's a price we are willing to pay for their freedom. Other families have their own boundaries and ways to use social platforms that work for them. But for us, the right amount is zero.

3. **Stop living on call** (unless you really need to be on call) and don't expect kids to be reachable at all times of the day and night. Every family has to set their own limits, but this is how it looks for our family:

- After a certain time of day, turn off the phone and put it in a cabinet. It's a retro way to use a cellphone—like we did in the early days of roaming charges and limited data.

- Have a landline for emergencies.

- No smartwatches—for grown-ups or for kids. Wearing a device, in my opinion, is like lugging around a mail bag of stress everywhere you go.

4. ***But what about safety?*** I know the motive behind giving young children phones and smartwatches is often to keep them safe. That's a good motive, so let's focus on what *will* protect children's well-being most of all. It isn't a line of constant, instant communication. It's freedom from that line. They need to be let off the hook, literally. *Distractedness* is dangerous. *Anxiety* caused by too many transmissions is dangerous. If we aren't sure what it looks like to let children exist without smartwatches, we just need to remember our own childhoods. Being out of touch with parents for reasonable chunks of time is good for developing independence. Situations like finishing practice early and needing a ride, leaving your lunchbox at home, breaking your skateboard and having to walk home—these are not emergencies; they are actually important classrooms for learning to solve problems without calling mom or dad. In the event of a true emergency, there are offline alternatives that might actually work faster and better. Every family should talk about strategies for what kids should do if they get lost, get hurt, or feel unsafe. We taught our kids these steps:

- Dial 9-1-1 on the landline if there is an emergency at home.

- Flag down a neighbor if you're out and about and need help.

- Take a loud whistle on a string when exploring the woods or canoeing at the lake.

In a real emergency, finding the nearest neighbor, calling EMS, or blowing an ear-shattering whistle is more likely to come in handy than mom and dad on the other end of a smartwatch.

5. ***Intercede.*** Our offloading mission needs the cooperation of parents, grandparents, teachers, camp leaders, mental health professionals, creatives, curriculum designers, tech developers, and those who influence governmental regulations. And it needs the fervent prayers of God's people who are following the lead

of our ever-present Guide and Helper. Consider one of these forms of action:

- Make fast media's burden on young people a theme in your church liturgy or your personal prayers. Ask for God's healing touch to break in and show us the way to protect young people. Ask for a divine infusion of courage to actually do the things he shows us.

- To raise awareness and rally collaborators, you might want to read through *Savoring Childhood* in a book club, church group, or school improvement council.

- Ask your school administrators and teachers to use analog ways to communicate assignments. It's not developmentally appropriate to expect young kids to navigate school email, Google Classroom notifications, and each teacher's digital notification system of choice. Parents can't do much to change this, except to let teachers and administrators know when it's too much. (Parents, if you don't actually know how much your kids receive in a day, ask them to show you.)

- Teachers, instructional designers, school board trustees, and principals: you have the power to put boundaries on the number of communications kids have to sift through. I so appreciated my son's fourth grade teachers sending home one Friday Flyer–on paper!– with announcements and assignments for the week ahead. Don't let the companies that make money off your subscriptions convince you that kids need to communicate on digital platforms when a homework journal or flyer announcement will do just fine.

Even though it might feel like a kind of deprivation to cut off some of the ways that our kids communicate digitally, it is a crucial step toward savoring childhood. Kids are depending on trustworthy adults to give them permission to ignore the cultural pressure to receive and respond to bags and bags' worth of digital mail. We must tell them—and show them—that it's okay to let it go.

Your intervention is an extension of God's mercy. So may the Holy Spirit give you the courage to step into the fray, the strength and wisdom to heft the mailbags up and out, the restraint to step back from your own bad habits, and the creativity to try something new.

10

Snail Mail

POSTCARD #1 CAME ABOUT SIX DAYS after we dropped our son at camp for the first time.

Dear mommy, daddy, and charlotte,

It's June 28, and i'm having <u>some</u> fun.

I'll tell you what I did when I get home.

Love, Henry

The postcard certainly did not offer a wealth of detailed information, but there was great rejoicing in the Pouch household when it arrived. Henry, who was nine at the time, was off at camp for fourteen whole days. At the six-day mark, we were missing him terribly and were very eager to know whether he was having a good time.

We had chosen this specific camp because of its rustic, old-school experience. Camp staff had warned us, only half-jokingly, that we wouldn't be getting any "proof of happiness" updates. No FaceTime. No texting. No camp-cam on a website for parental oversight. Not even phone calls. Campers can send and receive letters by mail. That's it.

So we sent Henry with blank postcards, paper, envelopes, and stamps, along with a list of family addresses—everything he would need to correspond with us by mail. Of course we had exchanged notes and cards with our kids through the years, but never before had we relied on the post as our only means for staying in touch. All of a sudden I was facing the slowness and suspense of waiting for mail. The postal service is not really all that slow, but in our age of instant messaging, traditional mail feels *glacial*. As a mom temporarily distanced from my young child, I felt like the slowness of the medium might just about do me in.

It was worth it, though. The snail mail policy at camp was clearly strategic. In order for kids to make deep connections with each other and savor the goodness of camp activities, they needed an unobtrusive mode of outside communication. Our kids have shared with us how isolating it is when their peers are glued to their devices. (You may have experienced that too!) At camp, *all* the kids would have their eyes and ears free of digital media so that they could communicate face-to-face. The atmosphere provided space for Henry to form connections with peers and counselors that transcended his typical school relationships. He was free to focus on exploring the wilderness and playing. His adventures also sparked a spiritual growth spurt, marked by independent Bible reading and a desire to talk with us about God and ask big questions.

Surprisingly, Henry's relationship with us deepened too. Even though we were apart, we were communicating in a new way by passing letters back and forth. I don't know if the camp leaders had this benefit in their strategic foresight, but it was a small rite of passage for Henry to be mostly *out* of touch with us. The chance to feel a little bit homesick can remind us how much we love and cherish each other. All of this would be enough without mail in the mix, but there's something about saying *I miss you* on paper that feels sturdy, special. Letter writing allowed both us and our son to give expression to these deep feelings.

Not that Henry's first postcard was especially deep. We had to work with him to develop letter-writing skills that could carry more substance. (I'll say more on that training process in a bit.) But even the postcard conveyed something most other media can't. The personality of handwriting. The erase marks and rewritten parts that

conveyed effort and thoughtfulness. And in forthcoming letters, records of his adventures and expressions of his love that we will keep
forever. This was a beautiful new wrinkle in our life together as a
family. Writing letters, it turns out, is a kind of training ground for
kind and meaningful communication.

SHALLOW, UGLY, IMPULSIVE, AND ROOTLESS

Digital communication is a training ground too. But not for kind and
meaningful interactions.

Instantaneousness is at odds with thoughtfulness. We have already
looked at the ways instant gratification can diminish stick-to-itiveness
and resilience, but here we see how immediacy as a design feature in
communications technology cheapens our interactions with one another. Missing punctuation and one-word answers might not be intentionally impolite choices, but this lazy communicating erodes
respect from our interactions both inside and outside the medium.
Capacity for warm and solicitous dialogue dwindles, and attention
spans shrink. I have found that the more time I spend on quick messaging platforms, the less patience I have for the speed of a normal
conversation. The training we get through our instant messaging has
created an epidemic of shallow listening. No wonder our relationships
lack depth these days!

Another casualty of high-speed, efficient messaging is the beauty
of words. Emojis, acronyms, and auto-fill sentences might be fine for
some situations, but the more we use them, the poorer our vocabularies become. Brevity can be beautiful, like a haiku. But when we rush
communication for efficiency's sake or out of habit, our communication appears ugly.

Fast media also breeds impulsivity. Many of us wouldn't dare to
write by hand the kinds of things we so easily tweet and text. Have
you ever fired off a digital response and regretted it? What might
have changed about the situation if you had written the message by
hand or delivered it face-to-face? Vulgar, rude, demeaning, and

threatening language pours into digital spaces from adults and children alike. Without built-in reflection space, we more easily dishonor one another.

It's not like creators and users of digital media deliberately set out to lower the quality of modern discourse. It's just that a medium's design unavoidably shapes its message. In this case, prioritizing speed shapes a message that cannot hold much depth, beauty, or forethought. And in turn, habitually sending and receiving those kinds of messages shapes *us* and our capacity for quality interactions. Half a century ago, media theorists like Marshall McLuhan and Neil Postman saw that modern media was poised to drown us in shallow content and gut our communication of eloquence and power.

For young people who've grown up with mostly app-ified modes of communication, their brains are wired up with totally different vocabularies, habits, expectations, and powers of attention. I don't want to sound anti-technology, but these tools are malforming our kids—at least the part of them that is made for deep and meaningful connection with other people and with God.

It is also worth noting that the ephemeral nature of digital media deprives us of tactile, physical memorabilia of the sort that nurtures a sense of rootedness and belonging. Have you ever tried to preserve something meaningful that came to you digitally? An elderly relative, now deceased, had a sweet, distinctive voice and always called me "Cuz." I wanted to hang on to a voice mail from him as a memento. But floating out there in data-storage neverland, alongside hundreds of other junky undeleted voice messages, his special one is hard to put my finger on. And that's the problem. We can't *put our fingers* on any of it. We've lost the physicality of correspondence. Perhaps we care less about our digital communications precisely because we know they aren't enduring. What a shame.

One of the things I have observed about young people today is a kind of haunted rootlessness—an insecurity about who they are and where they belong. Their lives are more documented than any previous generation—in the form of digital photos, e-documents, and biometric data. But that archive only exists as coded 0s and 1s floating in the ether of digital storage. It is not the kind of tangible evidence a person can place on a bedside table, turn to for daily reassurance, savor, smell, or take hold of in moments of loneliness or longing.

I believe our children are starving for solid artifacts of love. We might sneer at the sentimentality of old-timey communications—sending locks of hair or long love letters stained with candle wax and perfume—but I wouldn't be surprised if these ways of communication have a renaissance among the youngest generation who know, at some subconscious level, that these things form roots.

SLOWING IT DOWN WITH SNAIL MAIL

Physical notes and letters have the potential to combat each of these problems—shallowness, ugliness, impulsivity, and rootlessness.

In our previous chapter, we focused on reducing the *bulk* of digital comms to a human-friendly amount. Now we're going to look at cultivating *quality* communication by swapping digital messaging (at least some of the time) for the slow and thoughtful process of sending letters in the mail.

For generations, letters have been a crucial ingredient in maintaining strong relationships. Did you know that twenty-one of the twenty-seven books in our New Testament are letters? These letters are multipurpose. They are thoughtful responses to challenges and questions from the communities to whom they are addressed. They also include notes expressing love and gratitude to individuals and even little details about travel plans. The cherished correspondence was pastoral but also personal. For example, Paul begins his first letter to Timothy, "To Timothy, my true child in the faith: Grace, mercy, and peace from God the Father and Christ Jesus our Lord" (1 Timothy 1:2). The fact that these letters from two thousand years ago have survived proves that tender and meaningful written correspondence is worthy of preserving for posterity. I doubt our emails and texts will have that kind of lasting value!

Other nonbiblical, nontheological mail has survived the centuries as well. "What could be more pleasing to me than to write to you or to read your letters when I am unable to speak with you in person," wrote the Roman statesman Cicero in a letter to a friend. Mail has a *sacramental* quality—it is a visible reminder of intangible bonds and sentiments. A letter embodies the care of the person who went to the trouble to compose the message, and it bears traces of personality that no emoji or e-signature can show—idiosyncrasies in handwriting, distinctive stationery, characteristic words and phrases. It's no wonder that letters often become keepsakes.

Maybe you can remember getting mail as a child. I remember feeling especially loved and cherished whenever I received a letter addressed just to me or a handwritten note tucked in my lunchbox, my camp luggage, or my back-to-college suitcase. These were artifacts of care.

How do you think today's young people feel about the cultural tradeoff of snail mail for instant messages? I asked my kids this question, and they said they would much rather get "real mail" (as in physical letters) than texts or emails. "Real mail." That's an interesting choice of words, isn't it? And "real" communication is not only valuable on the receiving end. Creating and sending it is a uniquely powerful way to cultivate the disappearing art of conversation, which is key to "real" relationships.

Above all, practicing thoughtful written communication might be one of the most spiritually transformative practices to equip kids for a prayer-filled life. Quality communication is at the heart of "real" communion with God.

HOW TO PRACTICE SNAIL MAIL

To reclaim the benefits of snail mail, we don't have to completely quit faster forms of transmission. We just need to make the tradeoff

Snail Mail

often enough to reverse the crippling effects of fast media. I still text my friends to check in. I work remotely and rely on internet messaging to communicate with my colleagues for work. And I fully intend to continue forwarding Instagram reels with *Little Women* jokes to my sisters (classic!). But I know those things alone aren't strong enough to sustain deep relationships. We need more robust forms of communication for that. So how can we bring snail mail back into the rotation?

1. ***Create a homemade mailbox*** where kids can send and receive little notes between family members. This idea is not my own. I stole it from *Little Women* (two mentions in one chapter!); the March sisters put a postbox in the hedge to pass letters with young Mr. Lawrence. While this kind of mailbox isn't a Pouch family tradition, we have always enjoyed making notes for each other. Even toddlers and preschoolers can participate, as they learn to pour their hearts into a fingerpainting for Daddy or pencil scribbles for big sister. When kids begin to experiment with the alphabet, their spelling is adorably creative—sometimes so creative that you need them to tell you what it says. You may want to write their "translation" on the back if you plan to keep the note for the future.

2. ***When traveling,*** instead of calling or messaging while you or your child is away from home, try making snail mail your only mode of communication. It might give them (or you) some initial separation anxiety, but a few special letters could actually help you connect at a deeper level than if you were chatting digitally the whole time. If we want our kids to develop a more thoughtful and effortful habit of communication, we need to put in more effort ourselves and model how to do it. Don't bypass effort, because effort translates into care. So if you send a letter to your kid at camp, *don't type it!* And for heaven's sake, don't send a form letter made by someone else! It will be much more

memorable to your child if it has your own handwriting and your own thoughts.

3. *Try some training wheels.*

- Postcards are a great entry-level form of snail mail. A postcard's small space can feel less intimidating to a new writer. Early attempts might look like Henry's two-sentence postcard—which is totally fine. Again, the medium shapes the message, and postcards were designed for brevity. Even so, it is more mindful than instant messaging. That's a start, people!

- A next step in training for slow and thoughtful letter writing could be an interactive letter that guides the conversation for kids. I designed a fun letter to send to Henry at camp with blank spaces for his responses. I used drawings and words and invited him to fill it out with his own drawings and words and send it back to us. My hope was that it would prompt a bit more engagement than the postcard. And it worked! What he sent back gave us a tender and humorous glimpse into his experience. And I think it sparked a few ideas for what sorts of things he could include in his next letter to us.

4. *A neighborhood newsletter.* From time to time, our kids create a one-page newspaper for our neighbors to communicate tidbits of local information, share recipes, and announce things of interest, like a found kitten or an upcoming lemonade stand. William or I make copies of their handmade original and let them distribute the newsletter to homes around the block. It's just another way to nurture their sense of rootedness in our community and strengthen their analog communication skills.

5. *Display keepsake mail.* For children, a keepsake box or baby book can be a place to collect and display special letters. My mom was an excellent archivist of mementos from my growing up. We carried on the tradition with our kids. From the very first

Welcome, baby cards that came to each child, we have saved special correspondence over the years. Not everything on paper is keepsake-worthy, but even simple notes from teachers or birthday cards from friends help to chronicle relationships and make the bonds of love physically evident for young people. Adults can benefit from tangible mementos too. I like to hang letters on the refrigerator or set them on my desk where I can see them throughout the day. I also tuck special correspondence in my Bible sometimes if it contains something I want to pray about and revisit. A few letters of encouragement have been a grace to me as I've written this book. They are sitting beside me now. Just glancing at them reminds me of the people who love me, which spurs me on in my efforts.

6. ***Pen pals.*** Several families I know have a strong pen pal tradition. We haven't done this with the kids, but I'm leaning into it as an adult. Last year, I made a new friend at a retreat who immediately felt like a soul-companion. Not frequently, but every once in a while, Kate and I write letters to each other. It's really the only way we stay in touch. (I don't even have her phone number.) For some reason, snail mail just felt like the right way to continue to develop our friendship, and I've noticed that the letters hold a deeper level of connection.

7. ***Pause before responding.*** My sister introduced this practice to me as a way to carry over the benefits of snail mail into digital communications. Instead of responding right away to emails and texts, sit with the communication for a few hours or a day to prevent fast takes (misreadings, ungenerous interpretations) and to form a more thoughtful and thorough response. I like the idea of letting snail mail rub off on my e-habits rather than the other way around.

Pouring our hearts out isn't always natural or easy—with each other, or with God. But what a help it is to put things down in words, to move the thoughts from our heads to the page. As you step into the invitations of snail mail, you are teaching young people to communicate clearly, thoughtfully, and tangibly. You are expanding your child's ability to reach out to others and to you, and to enter deeper into a conversational friendship with the Lord.

11

Library Carts

Offloading

Snail Mail

Library Carts

Record Players

WHEN I WAS A KID, the pinnacle of my school year was the *Big Project*—whatever it happened to be for that year. Research projects awakened my God-given hunger for information—not the fast-facts kind of info that you could get in a trivia book (that was fun too), but intimate knowledge of a subject through deep investigation. I have a lifelong appreciation for the planet Venus and respect for the Algonquin peoples, thanks to elementary school research projects!

There was a particular pattern to the way my elementary school gave us access to information. The teacher would give the librarian a list of the students' names and the topics we had chosen for our projects. The librarian would then curate a small collection of books that were grade-level appropriate, high quality, and varied enough for the scope of our research, place them on a two-tiered metal cart, and wheel them down to our classroom. I took it for granted at the time—this act of expert curation. But it was a gift. It right-sized the library's vast collection for our developmental stage. Just a few resources were enough.

As I got older, I learned to make my way through the library shelves on my own, using the card catalog to search topically through what felt like an exciting breadth of content. I learned the index card method for collecting sources for a bibliography—and of course the number of sources my teachers expected me to reference gradually expanded as I aged up. For the most part, pursuing knowledge was slow and effortful. It took time to order a book through an interlibrary loan, to schedule an interview, or to wait for PBS to air a program. The parameters and tools given to us matched our developmental capacity so that the speed of information intake increased just enough to feel challenging and exciting but not overwhelming. It was a pace that allowed me to engage deeply with what I was learning.

ENTERING THE SHALLOWS

My freshman year of high school, Ask Jeeves unveiled an internet search bar. The librarians showed us how to type in a query and use parentheses to set off keywords. Then, we would wait for the dial-up connection to offer a few hits related to our inquiry. There were around a hundred thousand websites at the time. By my high school graduation in 2000, there were more than seventeen million.

It was the era of building and expanding the "information super-highway"—doesn't that sound exciting?

The term *superhighway* surfaced in several places simultaneously (Poland, Korea, the United States) and quickly became a buzzword. Everyone was so excited about the World Wide Web and the way it would speed up the rate at which humans access and share information. Why plod along at a library pace and learn within library limits when you can access millions of sources in seconds?

I think the internet optimists of those early years truly thought this rapid web expansion would be a gift to children. The whole world at their fingertips! Just imagine what kids might be able to learn and achieve.

Who could have envisioned back then how fast and expansive the superhighway would become? Today there are more than *a billion* websites, with close to four million added every day. And as predicted, the superhighway has revolutionized the way we access information. Aren't we all thoroughly conditioned now to cut straight to the internet search bar no matter what our query? It's the fastest tool with the broadest number of sources. So it must be the best, right? Certainly the internet has many benefits, but as it turns out, faster and broader isn't always better. Consider three documented consequences of the superfast, super-vast web that you've probably felt personally, and that particularly affect young people: shallow learning, overload, and getting lost.

Shallow learning. The web is an ocean of content, so it seems reasonable to assume that plunging into it will surely take us into the depths of information. But trying to engage with too many sources too quickly—especially low-quality sources—keeps us at the surface level of knowledge. The effect is that "we are becoming ever more adept at scanning and skimming, but what we are losing is our capacity for concentration, contemplation, and reflection." After noticing this phenomenon in himself, journalist Nicholas Carr sought out neuroscientific research to prove that using the internet literally changes the way our brains function. Pop-ups, invitations to click around, and links within links within links speed us from one source to the next, when we would usually be better off just sticking with one. Even the scrolling effect of reading on a screen (as opposed to turning pages) creates an "illusion of completeness" after the first few screenfuls of information. When we access information through the lightning-quick internet search bar, long-term memory formation and recall of learned material *decrease*.

Nicknamed "the Google effect," this rewiring of the way our brains store information should make us particularly worried about our children, whose brains are still developing. And yet e-learning methods and internet research are acceptable, even celebrated, alternatives to traditional teaching and learning. A tranquil deep dive into an ocean of beautiful information is not what the info superhighway offers us or our kids. Instead, as Carr famously titled his book, the internet is "The Shallows"—a paddle pool of soundbites and factoids that shrink our children's God-given capacity to think critically and remember things (capacities important for life with God and for general flourishing).

Overload. Retention is not the only thing that suffers when humans encounter too much information too quickly. Another consequence is psychosomatic distress. Cognitive overload affects people in different ways. Some feel angry, some feel depressed or anxious, some detach from the details that their brains are scrambling to process and passively give up on learning something new. Just ask any parent or teacher—these are responses that have skyrocketed as kids try to cope with the immense load of information and stimulation coming at them in today's high-speed, internet-connected world. Vast collections of data should be processed by computers, not children.

Getting lost. Sometimes it's fun to get lost—in the real world, in our thoughts, or in following our curiosity down the rabbit hole. But getting lost in the web's endless content isn't a healthy immersive activity. It can lead down dangerous pathways or simply cause kids to miss out on other beautiful life experiences.

We all know about protecting our kids from toxic content that is violent or inappropriate. But here's the thing about the internet: Even if we could block every image, word, and idea that isn't wholesome, the quantity and speed of its information can swallow up a healthy childhood. Jonathan Haidt points out that even when content is harmless, online engagement blocks crucial life experiences and fuels the mental health crisis. I once heard a teenager say, "*Toxic* means I lose myself." Not every child has reached that level of self-awareness. Not even every adult. But this is deep wisdom. When kids get sucked into the virtual world of information or entertainment, they can lose valuable chunks of childhood, and even their sense of self and purpose.

With every software update and every added terabyte of data storage, the information avalanche gains strength and speed. That means that the consequences of fast information will continue to grow worse unless we place limitations on our intake.

I know *limitations* sounds . . . well, limiting. Why would we ever withhold information from ourselves or from our children? One of the questions Jesus asked holds the answer. "What good is it if someone gains the whole world but loses their soul?" (Matthew 16:26 NIRV). The Good Teacher is letting us in on one of the most central truths for a flourishing life: The health and freedom of your soul is more valuable than *anything* you can acquire. Of course, this interior freedom hinges on much more than how we access information, but we must not ignore it as a critical factor.

Young people's relationship to information directly impacts whether or not they are spiritually free and alive. Every day, the choice to honor and nourish our souls and the souls of those in our care is made up of a million little decisions—even decisions about what to read, watch, and learn, how much content to consume, and how that content is delivered (if the actual delivery system has the power to rewire brains and warp desires). What good is it, then, to gain the whole world (wide web), if it forfeits something much more precious?

SLOWING IT DOWN WITH LIBRARY CARTS

In order to honor and protect our children's souls, we need to embrace reasonable limits on the range and speed of their info stream. We can't get rid of the internet—and if we use it well, we don't need to. Instead, what we need is a renewed approach, so that young people aren't encountering the *whole world* of information all at once at superhighway speed.

A slower user experience and a few quality sources can offer kids a more memorable, more enjoyable pace for learning. I want to take a cue from that elementary school librarian, God bless her, who took the time to whittle down a whole library of resources to one small cart of age-appropriate books. The library cart image stands out in my head as a symbol of trustworthy curation, a little monument to the beauty of wise and purposeful limits.

Applied in our lives and our kids' lives, library carts don't have to be literal buggies of children's books. The principle behind it is what I want to carry forward: A trustworthy guide selects a few sources, thoughtfully filtered for age-appropriateness and quality, in formats or presentations that support reflection rather than skimming. Library carts are simply curated collections of information resources. A curated collection isn't anti-internet, but it is much, much smaller and slower to use.

Part of my work as a content manager for Renovaré is to curate resources for a weekly newsletter. The newsletter is digital, powered and supported by the internet, but it isn't a wide-open gateway to the entire web—nor even to our entire archive of podcasts, articles, and books. That would be overwhelming and would certainly result in a shallow skim rather than a deep dive. Instead, the newsletter is a short list of resources—enough to provide a variety of angles, voices, and genres, but not too many to investigate in the course of a week. And crucially, the collection is handpicked by humans in conversation with the Holy Spirit. No algorithm can do that—converse with the Holy Spirit to select the right thing at the right time for a particular person or group.

There is something pastoral about curating resources. We can't rely on Google to do it in a way that safeguards hearts and minds. When you step into that role for the kids you love, you become a shepherd in the pattern of *the* Shepherd, who always guides his lambs with discretion and tenderness.

HOW TO PRACTICE LIBRARY CARTS

I'd like to propose three basic steps to library cart curation. It's a formula you can apply and adapt in a variety of situations:

Step One: **Narrow *the scope.*** Find the right number of items for your child to explore.

Step Two: **Vet *the sources.*** Make sure they are high quality and age-appropriate.

Step Three: Opt for **slow *media formats.*** Slower presentations support deeper engagement.

Here are a few examples of how William and I have practiced library carts for our kids and students over the years:

1. ***Curate Toys.*** For babies and toddlers, you can use the library cart principle to guide your selection of toys, manipulatives, and early books. Little ones take in information through sensory play and exploration, and just as with older kids, too much of a good thing can be overwhelming. Pull out just a few toys for little ones from the toy basket. Pick just one book off the shelf. Let toddlers practice putting the book back and choosing another one. One at a time is a good pace for books; two or three at a time for toys.

2. ***Get a set of vintage encyclopedias.*** Yard sales and local auctions are great; hand-me-downs are even better! Even though encyclopedias contain a wealth of information, a child's brain can engage better with the format of physical, bound volumes instead of fathomless data. When I was little, I loved looking through the set of 1950s encyclopedias in my grandparents' den. The vintage look of the illustrations was part of the appeal. It's cool to see an old map every once in a while, right? So don't worry if the set is several decades old; it can still be a wonderful container of kid-accessible info.

3. ***Ask for recommendations.*** Why not ask a real librarian? One of the best ways to put library carts into practice is to go to your local library and connect your child with a librarian who can serve as their guide to the vast (but not too vast) collection. You can also ask family and friends to recommend favorites. Charlotte probably reads forty or more books a year, so we solicit recommendations from family and friends to keep up with her appetite! I've also benefited from something called "reading upstream." Basically, if you read a book you love, the bibliography at the back of the book is like the author's own library cart prepared for readers who want to go deeper. The books and articles upstream

from the resource in your hand—the ones that flowed into and shaped the author's work—come pre-vetted and approved.

4. ***Print things out.*** I do this all the time, for the kids, and for myself. Reading something on paper eliminates clicking around with shallow retention or getting lost in the virtual world. And it enhances comprehension. A massive study of nearly half a million readers showed that young students had six to eight times higher comprehension when they read on paper than when they read the same material on a digital device. That's significant. If you care about the environmental impact of printing things (a good concern), keep in mind that paper is recyclable and can be sustainably sourced, whereas the resources used in digital screens and batteries are not.

5. ***Set the speed.*** When kids listen to information, say on a podcast or audiobook, help them set the speed to 1.0 (not 1.5x or double speed) to slow their intake to a pace that supports depth. (Grown-ups, this is good for us too!) When children are reading informational literature, teach them to slow it down by pausing at intervals to jot down notes, or maybe to highlight or underline as they go.

6. ***Interview a living person.*** People are my favorite slow resource. Asking someone they know and trust is a beautiful way for kids to find out information, but more and more we're bypassing face-to-face investigation because web research demands less time and less of our listening presence. How much learning and relational goodness is lost when we don't invest in conversations with our elders! Whether it's a formal interview or just a chat with granddad, an interactive conversation with a knowledgeable person has the power to stand out in a child's memory and to nurture a bond that feeds both mind and spirit.

Taking a library cart approach to resources is one way to protect kids from losing their depth, their sanity, and their freedom. And let's take a minute to look in the mirror. *Shallow retention. Information overload. Losing ourselves on the web.* Can adults be vulnerable to these problems too? Of course we can. Narrowing, vetting, and slowing are crucial disciplines for adults who want to engage more deeply with God's wonderful gift of information. Plus, it helps us model a healthy pace for our kids, and modeling is the best instruction we can give them.

The Maker of the mind and its magnificent capacity, the One who blesses us with the delight of discovery and the ability to pass knowledge on, the Source of every valuable conversation, book, documentary, podcast, and program, the Spirit who inspires creators and curators—our God—will be glorified when we carefully guard our children's hearts and minds by making all of these gifts accessible at the right pace and in the right proportion for their souls.

12

Record Players

THE ABILITY TO CAPTURE SOUND and share it widely is an amazing and beautiful human achievement. For most of human history, listening required being there, in person, to behold a sound at its emergence. Music, speeches, performances of various kinds—these auditory experiences existed only in the moment in which they were made, and then they were gone.

But with the invention of the phonograph in 1877, sounds could be *recorded* (engraved on a record) and experienced over and over again. And once radio was invented, sounds could be *transmitted* to listeners in different places. Each iteration of audio technology since these early days of sound engineering has made the listening experience a bit easier—and therefore a bit more prominent in daily life.

My first stereo was a clunky thing with AM/FM radio and a double tape deck. I can still remember waiting in my room for the Weekly Top 40 to come on, my finger hovering over the Record button so that I could add new songs to my mixtape of favorites.

By the time my younger sister was in middle school, no one had stereos that sat stationary in a room. They had portable CD players, or the newest tool at that time, MP3 players. Kids my sister's age had totally different habits of listening than my age group because they could so easily run, walk, and ride their bikes while listening.

Still, MP3 players had limits. They could only store audio tracks up to their memory limit. Now those limits have disappeared. With the dawn of internet streaming and wireless devices, people can listen anywhere, anytime, with endless possibilities to occupy their ears. For children today, sound is omnipresent.

THE COST

People have always been dazzled by the idea of limitlessness. We hate bumping into boundaries, endings, shortages. So we are forever inventing technologies that give us a sense of infinite possibility. But every new tool comes with a cost. I don't mean the price of the item (that too!). I mean there is always a downside—what it costs us, as individuals and as a society, to incorporate the latest invention into our lives. How it disrupts traditions and daily rhythms. How it shifts our expectations of one another. What or who gets left behind. The toll it takes on our attention. And, crucially, how it fools us into thinking that we don't need God.

To truly judge how valuable a particular technology is, we need to ask: *What is it costing us, and is it worth it?*

I wonder if we've paused to ask that question about today's audio technology. Yes, the newest technology demolishes the limits of previous tools. It has revolutionized our listening habits. But at what cost?

If we consider that question bearing in mind that we hope to cultivate an attentive, with-God life for ourselves and for our children, here are a few things we must consider:

- As luxurious as it feels, on-demand listening eliminates waiting— costing us a natural training space for patience and gratitude.

- Handheld devices are *personal* tools, optimized for private listening, which comes at the cost of connection. What used to be a communal activity is more likely these days to be individual, robbing kids of the joy of sharing the experience.

- The Cloud—that practically unlimited trove of data storage accessed through the internet—dangles so many options in front of users that we are taking in music and other audio content in record-breaking proportions. The price? We have no silence for deep focus, reflection, or prayer.

These are costs that can bankrupt a soul.

The phrase "ears to hear" appears at least sixty times in the Bible. "Whoever has ears, let them hear," Jesus repeatedly warns. The famous saying has many implications, but one important takeaway is that possessing the physical capacity to process sound isn't the same thing as *paying attention*. Ears can be preoccupied by too many noises and desensitized so that they miss the things worth hearing. Kids growing up in the era of constant auditory stimulation can be so caught up in their own personal listening experience that they miss the sounds around them in nature and conversation, and they miss the opportunity for silence.

This tradeoff is devastating. It means losing a whole interior world of pondering and appreciating, of processing and formulating thoughtful responses. It means being desensitized to the way God can use sound waves (and the absence of sound waves) to communicate. Without some breaks in the stream of media, it is very hard for children to notice the thoughts and impressions that carry the still, small voice of the Lord.

They have ears . . . but their ears are too preoccupied to hear.

SLOWING IT DOWN WITH RECORD PLAYERS

I have fond memories of great audio in my early years, BCP (before cell phones). I remember my dad's jazz music while he painted, and his Bible on cassette collection. I remember my mom's Chaka Khan album—fantastic dance music. My siblings and I had a favorite record of Christmas songs that we still talk about. I can recall particular radio hits that I associate with a memorable youth group trip or school dance. And one of my earliest memories is being about three years old and listening to storybook read-along tapes on my Fisher-Price tape player. Each recording started out with, *When you hear the chime, turn the page! Rrrrring!*

But I also remember a lot of space in between these media experiences—space where no sound was playing in the background besides the natural sounds of my surroundings. People's voices, my grandmother's piano, the sounds of the outdoors while we played. It was a gift to grow up without the monolithic presence that audio media has become.

I believe we can get back to that, at least within our own homes. One of the easiest shifts we can make to slow the stream so that our children's ears are free to hear again is to swap out portable, internet-connected devices for older technology with helpful limits. Record players, for example, are excellent tools for listening without over-whelming children's ears. On her fourteenth birthday, we gave Charlotte a record player and a few of our favorite vinyl albums. I'm drawn to vintage things, but it wasn't primarily nostalgia that motivated this gift. It was the design of the technology itself.

First of all, a record player isn't portable. It can't go in my daughter's pocket or come with us in the car. Over the years, tech wizards have probably made billions of dollars making music mobile, giving users the freedom to listen everywhere. But we choose different freedoms for our kids. Freedom to strike up a conversation, to notice subtle sounds like wind and birds and whispers. Freedom to hum their own tune and make their own music some of the time. And freedom to experience the absence of sound that encourages deep thinking.

Another built-in boundary of vinyl is that it doesn't play automatically or effortlessly. Telling Siri, "Play Earth, Wind & Fire" is convenient, but too much convenience kills patience and perseverance, as we discussed in the Slow Gratification section. If we apply the principles of slow gratification to our media consumption, we can see how a record player reactivates intentionality and effort. Thumbing through albums, selecting one, pulling it *gently* out of its sleeve, placing it on the turntable, pressing Start (or dropping the needle if your player is really old-school), and carefully putting the record away when you are finished—these are small movements; nothing complicated, to be sure. But even little efforts make us more mindful about what we're doing. Slowing the stream of media with a reasonable amount of *in*convenience helps kids learn to savor the process more than if they get it instantly.

Third, a record has a natural end. With streaming technology, you can listen on and on forever. Not so with a record. Typically, you listen to a full side (usually in the order that the musician or producer designed). Once that side has played, you can flip it and listen to the other side. Then you have finished the record. Of course, you can play it again or manually skip around, but you must actively *choose* to do so. It's important to help our kids exercise volition and self-control instead of consuming media mindlessly. And it's good for things to have an end! A natural stop gives a child's ears a chance to come up for air and grow comfortable with sound's absence.

It isn't just the album itself that has an ending. A collection of records is finite and physical. Older listening technologies often stored tracks on things that you could see and touch—records, cassettes, CDs. You could fathom the scope of content in front of you. Streaming technology, in contrast, obscures the volume of data. Digital content still requires storage (which has an astronomical and growing price tag), but it's in some data center far away—out of sight, out of mind, and incomprehensibly vast.

The collection of data that we call the Cloud is practically endless, and this is bewildering to the human system, especially a child's. The ability to listen to anything under the sun and never hear the same thing twice might sound fun, but in reality, limits are a kindness to our children. A smaller scope of options prevents a sense of overwhelm. And normalizing a finite collection of options to enjoy again and again builds contentment, which is natural immunity to the pathogens of greed and discontent.

Finally, record players and older technologies tend to be more group-friendly. In my mom's generation, kids took their favorite 45s to friends' houses to listen together, swap, and share. Sharing digital music is not as interactive. And the isolating functionality of headphones makes listening a solo experience even if listeners are physically together. Author Marva Dawn said that we have technologized our intimate moments and become intimate with our technology. Is there anything sadder than seeing two kids together, both wearing headphones and *not* communicating?

Solitary media consumption can cause or intensify feelings of isolation. With the staggering rise of loneliness and depression, especially among young people, we might want to rethink any of our habits that block social interaction and draw children into themselves. One benefit of old-school technology like the record player is that it is built to make listening a more social experience. It helps families create a ritual around sharing favorite music rather than each member living inside the bubble of their own self-curated soundtracks all the time.

HOW TO PRACTICE RECORD PLAYERS

In our household, we have transitioned almost exclusively to records, because we see a record player's limitations as a gift to ourselves and especially to our children.

But you certainly don't have to have a record player to lean into healthier, slower listening habits. Swapping out digital tools for a record player is just one example of how to place boundaries on audio intake in order to cultivate a listening life. Below are some suggestions for other boundaries you can use to reduce the pace and prominence of audio media, and I'm sure you'll come up with some creative experiments of your own.

1. ***Give kids a break from headphones.*** Headphones block out most of the world's sounds and privatize listening. There's a time and a place for headphones, but try giving your kids a month or longer without them and see if it frees up their ears for other kinds of listening. In our experience as parents and teachers, William and I have observed that kids are more tuned in to good things in the world, more connected to peers, and generally happier when they don't have headphones on.

2. *Make it stationary.* Most media tools now are designed to travel around with you, but portability makes listening mindless and distracting. To encourage better listening habits, try keeping technology grounded in fixed physical locations. A TV in one room, a record player in another, a specific place for the Bluetooth speaker. Even if it was made to travel, you can keep it anchored in one spot. Enjoy using it in the area you designate, and let yourself roam free from A/V technology in the other areas of your home, yard, and beyond.

3. *Build limited collections of content.* Records are great, but there are other options like vintage cassette players with used tapes (eBay!), or the screen-free Toniebox. Make it normal to have just a *few* options (records, tapes, Tonies) that your child can listen to over and over again. I know that can be monotonous for the adult in the room, but repetition is good for learning and forming roots through memories and favorites.

4. *Listen to what your kids are listening to for one whole day,* even if it annoys you. Think of it as research about what they are putting in their ears—like you might track your child's food intake to ensure they're getting enough good stuff. What did you notice?

5. *Try an audio media fast.* Take a day (or an hour, or a twenty-minute drive to the store) to pause all audio media. Do you feel free? Anxious? Bored? Make note of your internal resistance and other things that bubble to the surface as you experiment.

6. *Make your own music.* Model and encourage singing, playing instruments, humming, clapping, and whistling. Making music only happens if there's a lull in the stream of audio media, so turning off the piped-in audio sets the stage. You can also set the stage by making instruments accessible. My grandmother kept a cardboard box in the hall closet that she called the rhythm band box. It had an assortment of instruments suitable for the youngest grandchild all the way up to the oldest great-granny. Maracas, triangles, handheld drums, tambourines, and—perhaps the most underrated instrument of all—sticks. Give a kid a pair of rhythm sticks and I guarantee they'll start tapping a beat!

It's so easy to listen to anything and everything, and so hard to keep our ears open to the things that really matter. But in truth, we have more control over what goes in than we take advantage of. These are powerful but small steps to win back your child's freedom to pay attention to the things that matter, to give them back their "ears to hear."

PART 4

Slow Consuming

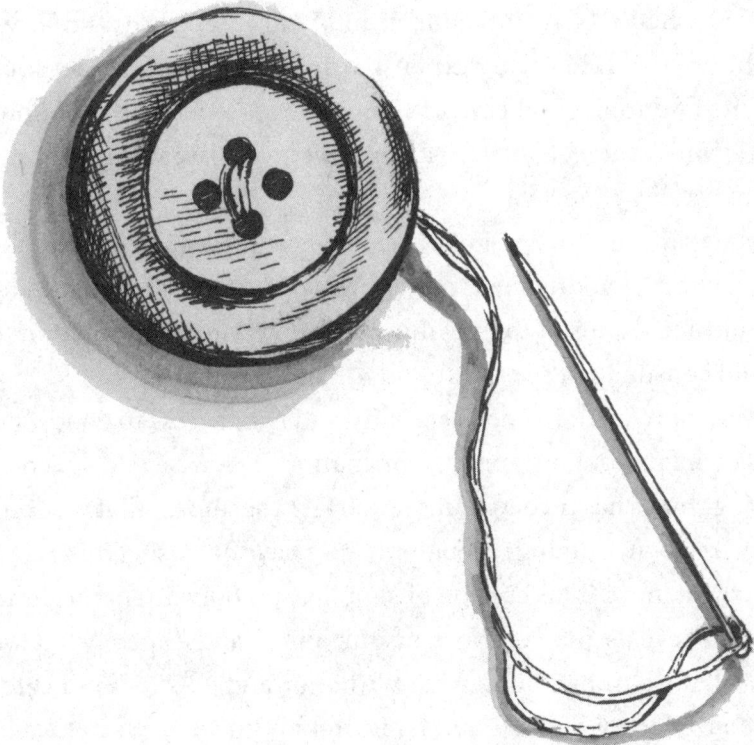

MY GRANDMOTHER GRACE WAS a child during the Great Depression. Her father, a grocer, went bankrupt giving food to customers on credit. I would never wish for myself or my children the financial hardship that Grandmama's generation lived through, but I do admire the formative effect that such a childhood had on her slow and respectful use of things. She saved wrapping paper, rubber bands, and aluminum foil. She chewed Wrigley's gum half a piece at a time. There weren't many toys for us grandkids at her house, but Grandmama made her own fun with stories, music, and word games. She had a beautiful collection of carvings my grandfather made by hand, but few truly expensive items. She kept clothes for a long time and took good care of them. She shopped with coupons, cooked from scratch, and almost never went out to eat. And yet she was remarkably generous.

Maybe you can think of someone who is your shining example of simpler living. Grandmama is mine. Her slower way of buying, using, and disposing stands out in my mind as a powerful contradiction to the rapid consuming I see all around me, and within me.

Our era of relative financial stability and easy access to goods has had its own far-reaching spiritual formation. The ease and speed of acquiring things has turned us into such fast consumers that we don't think twice about blitzing through what we have or tossing things out. We'll just get more. This erosion of simplicity in outward habits influences and reveals the contours of our inner landscapes—what we desire, what we think about, what we honor and adore. It indicates that we are deeply divided and confused about what matters, and that division taints our outlook on everything from how we operate businesses and vote for policies to what we talk about around the dinner table.

Kids absorb subtle messages as they experience fast-paced, unchecked consumerism. And the message is this: Well-off means having all the food, entertainment, vacations, clothes, cars, gadgets, home goods, jewelry, and houses that a person could want. True happiness lies in the ability to spend freely, without limitations, and to blow through resources and replace things without consequence.

Pope Francis said that "throwaway culture" warps our outlook not only toward the environment and toward purchased goods, but also toward people. If we think using things up for our own pleasure is acceptable, we will be more likely to use and throw away friendships, shop for churches, and even treat fellow human beings as commodities to serve our own ends. What a sad departure from God's kingdom ethic of love! Caring for people and creation is meant to be a wonderful vocation that each of us, young and old, contributes to in our own unique ways. But fast consuming comes from and reinforces a "me first" ethic in us, which we pass on to our young people. The cycle will repeat itself unless we can slow our consuming way, way down.

I believe we can, with God's help. It might not be in sweeping reform, but every small step matters.

Let me tell you about a funny failure (or at least not a glowing success story) from our experiments with slowing down consumption. When I first heard that cloth diapers were making a comeback, I was pregnant with our second child. In theory, I loved the idea of switching from disposable pampers to these new and improved washable diapers. I didn't want to add a swimming pool–size load of trash to the landfill. I was sold on the idea of being better stewards of our money and the earth's resources by taking a harder, more sustainable way.

A friend who had used cloth diapers with her kids showed me how they work: an outer layer with snaps keeps everything contained, and an absorbent insert goes underneath to do the hard work (quite advanced compared to the old safety pin method of long ago). She talked me through the dunking, scraping, and spraying, and still I was somehow convinced by her testimony that this would be an easy switch from our previous experience with disposable diapers. Sealing the deal, I found a set of top-brand cloth diapers in good condition at a secondhand kids' clothing sale. I could only afford to buy the bare minimum number recommended for keeping the laundry circulating. But I felt confident and really proud of myself for saving the earth. Pride cometh before . . .

That fall, Henry was born. When I jumped on the cloth diaper train, I hadn't taken into account that our laundry machines were in the basement. With no inside access. We had to go out the front door, down the steps, and through a barn-style door to get to the dark, damp room where the washer and dryer were. And as it turned out, the outside snapping layer of the diapers couldn't go in the dryer, so we installed a clothesline. And then came winter. Very quickly, we were disenchanted with the cloth diapers.

We seemed to run out of clean ones every day, even though we were doing laundry constantly. William ended up doing most of the work, and since I had surprised him with the big decision to switch, I felt really bad about how hard it was. I'm not exaggerating when I say we spent hours and hours a week stuffing inserts, unstuffing inserts, soaking liners, washing, hanging, and folding these dang diapers. We made it to about eleven months and finally gave up.

I share this to admit that I am no great wizard at living waste-free. As I move into the chapters ahead with our little victories and suggestions for making and mending, sharing and simplifying, I know that they are tiny steps. I am still learning, and I have a long way to go as I open my daily rhythms and perspectives to Jesus' transforming influence. But I want to encourage you with the reminder that every little bit helps. The worst thing we can do is convince ourselves that small efforts are too small to count, and that we might as well just succumb to not trying at all.

I say try anyway. Try and fail. Even if you only go eleven months with something hard and hate it all the way, it's not really a failure if it shifts your balance ever so slightly from wasting toward saving, if it makes you more mindful of what you use, and if it forms something good in your soul (even if it's humility!). God is with us even in our baby steps and backward steps toward taking on the inward character of Christ. So don't toss the possibility of change out with the trash. Your little steps are worthwhile.

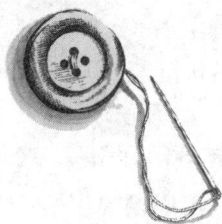

13

Simple Tastes

WE CELEBRATED WILLIAM'S FORTIETH BIRTHDAY last year with an extravagant night out. At a posh Italian restaurant overlooking the park, we had oysters and champagne, followed by grilled bread with ricotta and honey, and our main course was duck (William's favorite treat). We left the restaurant and strolled two blocks down Main Street to the theater. From our box seats we had a premium view of our favorite jazz musician in concert. It was a magical night of food, music, and a little taste of luxury.

As amazing as that celebration was, a different party ranks even higher in my catalog of favorite moments. It was our thirteenth wedding anniversary, and we had just moved into our hundred-year-old house. Nothing was renovated yet. It was summer in South Carolina, and the house didn't have air conditioning. We were insanely hot and discombobulated. Our dishes were still in moving boxes. Every nook and cranny of the house was in a state of disorder or disrepair. House-poor and exhausted, I squashed any thought of splurging on an anniversary celebration.

But Charlotte and Henry decided to make the day special for us in their own way. In the disheveled kitchen, Charlotte somehow found cake pans and started secretly making an anniversary treat. William and I were upstairs installing some blinds when Henry burst in to announce that we must "get fancy in wedding clothes right away!" So William put on a tuxedo jacket (with shorts), and I squeezed into my wedding dress and put on some costume jewelry.

We followed Henry down to the shabby screened porch to find the picnic table set with paper plates and a jar of flowers cut from the yard. The porch was embellished with hand-drawn signs and bows from the gift wrap drawer. And the crown jewel was a miniature wedding cake, baked and decorated by Charlotte.

Sitting there sweating in my wedding dress, eating cake baked by a nine-year-old off a paper plate, I felt completely content. It was the simplest of celebrations and also one of the sweetest.

CHAMPAGNE TASTES

I do not intend to suggest to you that the first party I described above—the fancy dinner and concert—is unholy. But I do want to contrast the two experiences as pictures of "the good life" and suggest that too much of the first kind of pleasure—the flashy, expensive kind—can desensitize us to the goodness of homespun festivities.

Wants tend to snowball, don't they? The more we focus on getting, the more our emotions and impulses reflect "the nervousness and fury of acquisitiveness." There is a powerful illusion that gaining will bring us closer to contentment, but once we have dedicated the bulk of our attention and energy to acquiring, acquisition itself has become our love. "We have given our hearts away," to quote Wordsworth. And this is exactly what Jesus said would happen: "Where your treasure is, there your heart will be also" (Matthew 6:21).

If losing one's heart to the false god of materialism was a threat in the time of Jesus, you can bet it's still a threat today in our wealthy, consumer-centered society. Just think about the question "What makes a childhood *good*?" The first criteria that jump into most people's minds are material blessings: economic stability, affording the best schools and extracurricular experiences, trips to Disneyland, toys, clothes, braces, cars, college, blowout birthday parties. But what about intangibles? None of those bought experiences can substitute for the greatest parts of childhood: a loving family, time in nature, time with God, memories, stories, friendships, and so on.

Jesus began his most famous sermon by explaining what makes someone well-off by God's standards (Matthew 5:1-12; Luke 6:20-23). His description of a good life surprised his audience then, and it still challenges us today. The people he identified as blessed were actually those whose experiences of hardship set them free from the illusion that contentment lies in acquisition, ease, power, and popularity. The poor, those who mourn, those who desperately long for justice, and the persecuted usually have a clearer perspective on treasures of the heavenly sort, like truth, love, belonging, spiritual gifts, and shalom.

"But woe to you who are rich," Jesus continued (Luke 6:24). Counting on material possessions to satisfy you is a losing game. It substitutes something consumable for the imperishable joy of a with-God life and breeds ambition, greed, anger, and jealousy. This is how a heart comes to be ruled by money rather than by God. Of course, not every person with financial means is ruled by money. (I am thinking of wealthy friends who bless others out of their means. And people with middle or low incomes can be just as self-centered and money-obsessed as rich folks.) But Jesus is pointing out that people who live like kings in this world are more susceptible to giving their hearts to the love of money.

Whole books have been written on the subject of Jesus' blessings and woes, so I humbly offer my thoughts on how Jesus' sermon can help us rethink our image of a good childhood:

- Having less can actually help kids be content.

- Materialism is a false value system that ignores the deepest needs of the human soul.

- True joy comes not from external conditions, but from receiving God's love and becoming the kind of person who can freely love God and others without selfishness getting in the way.

SLOWING IT DOWN WITH SIMPLE TASTES

The good news is that there are ways to help kids cultivate a palate for the things that Jesus calls good. "Champagne tastes" are acquired. So are simple ones.

A child's concept of the good life can be straightened out later in life, but the best-case scenario is to shape appetites from the start that will guide kids in a healthy direction now and in the future. Whether you have young children who are just beginning to conceptualize these ideas or older teens and young adult kids who have already absorbed a lot of messages, just remember that tastes are malleable.

Take a good look at your children. What do they love? What do they naturally turn to for comfort? Which of your child's existing desires already align with God's heart?

A few years ago, Charlotte filled out a questionnaire for camp that asked, "If you had twenty-four hours completely free, what would you do with the time?" Here is her response (shared with her permission):

> I would wake up early, make myself a hot breakfast, and then ride my bike to a beautiful lake. I might bring my watercolors to paint a landscape picture. I would come home and read a good book for a couple of hours. I would play through all my favorite piano pieces. After that, I'd bake cookies and snuggle up in our den to watch home movies with my family. Then I would eat butter noodles for supper and have warm brownies as my dessert. I would eat brownies all night until I fell asleep on the couch.

When Charlotte was much younger, one of her teachers gave a similar prompt as a journal assignment. Students were to draw a heart on their page and fill it with happy words. Then outside the heart, students could write about things they dislike. Inside Charlotte's heart, she had written: *reading, cats and kittens, storms, God, art, family, shopping, ice cream, twice-baked potatoes, Easter, friends, Christmas, church, travel.* Conspicuously written outside the heart were the words *bird poop* and *tights* (which made it crystal clear how much she hated wearing tights).

Sometimes just asking our children what makes them happy can give us great clues about the free, renewable sources of delight that our children already value—like family time, reading, music, and the beauty of nature. And as with Charlotte's descriptions, listening to our kids can help us to become aware of their consumer-focused desires. Before analyzing too quickly, simply notice.

Next, you can begin to gently mold those appetites by feeding the tastes that will serve your children well and subduing the ones that could escalate into unhealthy fast-consuming habits. The material items and pricey experiences that a child might crave aren't necessarily things we need to withhold, but my approach is to make those things rare treats. (And occasionally my kids make requests that I will never gratify, for their own good.) The point is that when we slow down consuming and play up other sources of enjoyment, we strengthen our kids' ability to find contentment in simplicity.

Relativism is one of the sneakiest contributing factors to fast consumption. Children's ideas about what is normal are warped by what they see other people doing. In the same sermon where Jesus preached about blessings and woes, he repeatedly used the phrase "You have heard that it was said . . . but I say to you . . ." (see Matthew 5). Our world is constantly sending us the message that we must spend and accumulate more and more. We have heard it said that this is the way to find contentment. But Jesus tells a different story. A powerful way to encourage simple tastes is to expose kids to countercultural examples of generous ownership and slow spending that confront the insanity of consumerism and offer them a new vision of normal—one where Jesus is the standard-setter.

HOW TO PRACTICE SIMPLE TASTES

In many ways, my children have been my teachers about what really matters in this life. Very young children naturally have simple tastes.

They want to be hugged. They delight in everyday wonders. They care nothing about impressing others with their net worth or storing up for the future. I want to share with you some practices that have helped us to continue cultivating that childlike clarity about what really matters (and what doesn't):

1. ***Burst the bubble.*** If you live in a community of fast-paced, unchecked consumerism, it can really skew your child's sense of what is normal. Of course we can't choose our children's friends for them, but we can nurture relationships with friends whose families live modestly. This is not about assessing someone's net worth or judging anyone for their lifestyle—people can live modestly at every income bracket. This is about finding solidarity with those who have similar values about the good life. Another way to help shape a child's ideas about what is normal is to expose them to different pockets of society in your city. Even going to a grocery store in a different part of town can be eye-opening in a good way. These kinds of encounters help drive home Jesus' message that the poor can teach us—and that requires our proximity.

2. ***Scaled-down parties.*** Every once in a while, a Pinterest-perfect party or lavish celebration can be fun, but I've noticed that the standards keep escalating. For kids, the truly memorable ingredients of a birthday or holiday celebration are togetherness and play, and those ingredients are free. Instead of thinking in terms of what to *buy* when you plan the next party, think about what you already have. Do you have a tent? Invite three or four friends to camp out in the backyard—hotdogs and s'mores are all you need! Have a bunch of sports equipment? Host a mini Olympics birthday party in the park, and play relay race games. Homemade, creative decorations—like the ones Charlotte and Henry made for us that special anniversary—are even better than store-bought decor. Flowers or greenery from the yard,

candlelight, and music—there are many ways to turn up the volume on cheerful times together without spending anything.

3. *Physical closeness.* What a wealth of joy God gives us through touch and attention! Notice the power of touch in this scene from Mark's Gospel: "People were bringing children to him in order that he might touch them, and the disciples spoke sternly to them. But when Jesus saw this, he was indignant and said to them, 'Let the children come to me; do not stop them. . . .' And he took them up in his arms, laid his hands on them, and blessed them" (Mark 10:13-16). Though physical closeness can be commodified, it is meant to be freely available to each and every human. Offer your child a variety of experiences like holding a baby, receiving and giving lots of hugs, sitting in grandparents' laps, passing the peace of Christ with hand-shakes at church, and being close to you—in the same room, rather than isolated so much of the time. Physical closeness has a surprising ability to touch kids' hearts with a sense of well-being and joy.

4. *Repetition.* A taste for what's next and what's new can be subdued by practices that normalize repetition and reuse. Something as simple as eating the same basic ingredients for lunch every day for a week can break an escalating appetite for more and more specialty foods. At our house, we stay away from one-time-use activities and toys (the happy-meal type games that go in the trash after you use them). And another way we've nurtured repetition is to let long-running interests keep going as long as they will. Don't feel you need to press your child to take on a new hobby or new plaything just for the sake of some-thing new. Children don't get tired of doing the same thing over and over again. (Sometimes we might wish they would!) If we could learn from little ones to delight in repetition, we would find our lives much simplified.

5. ***Stories that shape values.*** Jesus consistently used stories to shape his disciples' understanding of a good life. The Bible is the best of all stories for tuning kids' hearts to his values. But fiction and historical stories are also wonderful for modeling others-centered love. A few of our favorites for kids at various stages are the books *Little House on the Prairie* and *A Christmas Carol* and the movies *It's a Wonderful Life* and *The Boy Who Harnessed the Wind.*

6. ***Borrow books.*** Once or twice a month, William takes our kids to the public library—one of our society's most beautiful civic systems, and a shining counterpoint to the twisted American dream of *owning* everything. We do own books, mostly ones we've read over and over again, but if it's a one-time read, we prefer to borrow. Borrowing books is a great way to shape a vision for borrowing and lending other things as well: sports equipment, camping equipment, baby gear, suitcases, clothes, tools, and so forth. We can easily share many of these among neighbors, family, and friends. The bloated ownership of our lifestyles is insanity when you realize how much could be shared.

Your life is one of the most impactful stories your kids will read as they decide whether or not to trust Jesus' surprising, wonderful, and challenging message about the good life. When my "champagne tastes" get too demanding, my favorite way of returning to God's truth about what matters is to get away from the marketplace completely and soak myself in nature's un-ownable, immeasurable beauty, or to step away from adult concerns like bills and groceries and home improvements to simply play with my children. These are little ways to keep my own appetites for getting and spending in check and to reconnect with the Giver of all, who has the power to revive my delight in the simple things of life whenever it dips low.

The apostle Paul wrote, "I have learned the secret of being content in any and every situation, whether well fed or hungry, whether living in plenty or in want" (Philippians 4:12 NIV).

I want to learn that secret too—learn it at the deepest level and pass it on to my dear ones.

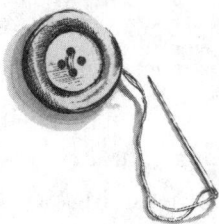

14

The Creative Option

YESTERDAY I PUT AN AMAZON-SOURCED CAT HOUSE on the curb next to the trash can. It is essentially a cardboard box with a fleece-wrapped lid. There's a sisal scratch pad on one side, an entry hole on the other, and a puffball dangling from a cheap piece of rope.

This is probably the tenth in a long succession of cat accoutrements I have bought for our lone pet, Jasmine—part of an ongoing mission to get her to stop clawing the sofa. The cat has rejected every single one. Within a few weeks of purchase, each feline playhouse has been abandoned to the curb for requisition or disposal.

Both of my grandfathers had wood shops where they constructed small household items, and both of my grandmothers sewed and knew how to make things. But me? Oh, I'm just over here spending hundreds of dollars on cat contraptions that my fifth grader could have built with a hot glue gun.

Like a typical twenty-first-century person with Amazon one-click purchase power, I often forget that there is an alternative option to purchasing everything ready-made. The buy-use-repeat cycle is so ingrained in our cultural patterns and so habit-hardened that I usually participate in it without even noticing. Until the tenth cat box goes on the curb, and I suddenly realize that this is not a sane way to live.

How did we get to this point—this end user identity and this pattern of rapid, mindless consuming? And how can we slow it down for the sake of savoring childhood?

THE END USER GOSPEL

Without wading far beyond my depth into the sea of economics, I want to simply observe that the problem of fast consuming is most rampant in societies where a focus on maximizing profits is accepted as the absolute, unquestioned ideal of business. I'm not talking about making a living; I'm talking about ruthlessly accumulating wealth and buying in to a worldview that says the good life is all about being an end user.

Business models like that have a vested interest in distancing us from the practical can-do attitude that our grandparents had. The Boy Scout merit badge library from 1965 offered more than a hundred pamphlets for gaining knowledge and proficiency in everything from foraging to printing, basket weaving to pigeon raising. Varied and advanced, the list looks otherworldly compared to things kids spend time doing today. Commenting on this stark contrast, cultural critic Ted Gioia writes, "You earned [a merit badge] by going out into the world and developing some new skill in dealing with it. So you might learn fishing, climbing, gardening, first aid, photography, archery, rowing, backpacking, and a bunch of other things. Those were the apps before we had apps. . . . This is the real world. This is how you develop confidence and mastery in it."

In a world where the ultimate life goal is being an end user, Scout badge skills no longer serve a purpose, other than perhaps as obscure hobbies. So at the stage of childhood when kids in previous generations were learning to contribute to their families, churches, and communities, young people today are mastering levels of video games or curating their social media image.

Kids are not makers and doers anymore. They are clientele. And perhaps we think that's a good thing. We might think we are sparing kids from drudgery and hardship by eliminating labor from their lives and focusing on keeping them entertained. However, consuming rather than contributing takes a toll. Despite being more entertained than ever, a rising number of children today (9 percent of sixteen- to twenty-five-year-olds in one study) say that they "feel they have nothing to live for." As one Gen Zer put it, "We are no longer embedded in a community to which we contribute . . . we have absolutely no institutional sources for acquiring wisdom available for us, and lastly, we are bombarded with b***s**t (in the technical sense of the word)." I wouldn't have expressed this in exactly the same terms, but I feel it resonating in my soul. Even kids who have been thoroughly conditioned to see themselves as mere consumers seem to sense that there must be an alternative. And indeed there is.

SLOWING IT DOWN WITH THE CREATIVE OPTION

The alternative to an end user childhood is so enjoyable, so naturally kid-friendly, and so good for the soul that I can't wait to dive into it with you! It is to reconnect our children with their creative potential.

Philosopher Dallas Willard writes, "The true person is not a consumer, but a creative will. We are designed to be creators, initiators, not just receivers." This is not a wholesale prohibition against consuming. (We have to consume to live!) But it's a reminder that we are not *just* consumers, and neither are our kids. To be made in God's image is to share in a heritage that is essentially creative.

The first person described in Scripture as being filled with the Spirit of God was a man named Bezalel—an artist whom God commissioned shortly after the exodus to build the tabernacle and to fill it with decorative elements that would give the people a "continual vision of God throughout their wanderings in the wilderness." It was a massive undertaking, and Bezalel was the equivalent of general contractor, chief interior designer, artist, and craftsman all rolled into one (Exodus 31:2-5). It is fascinating that the term "filled with the spirit" is, as Richard Foster points out, "first used, not of a priest or prophet or patriarch, but of an artisan, a 'blue collar' worker." Perhaps "this will give us a hint of how much God values the work of our hands."

Not everyone is a Bezalel, but each of us has the capacity to contribute. That's not the message our children get when we let them be "bombarded by b***s**t," as the young man put it. Underneath that pile of amusement and passive consuming, there's a buried alternative. And with a little digging, we can resurface it for the next generation.

I would like to suggest a few commitments we can make in our families and communities to bring the creative option back to the light.

Commitment one: Honor the value of handmade things. As a Sunday school teacher and music therapist for hospitalized children, my grandmother was well known for her homemade flip charts for leading songs. She wrote the songs in cursive lettering on a big pad of paper and turned the pages manually. Just think what an anomaly handmade things are for childhood today. At church and school, they get mostly professionally printed handouts, computer-generated graphics, and high-tech video presentations. At home, most of the items kids play with, wear, and see in their home environments are mass-produced and bear little to no trace of human craftsmanship. In this fast-production, fast-consumption landscape, kids absorb the message that machine-made and "professional" items are superior to those made by people they know and love. Nothing could be further from the truth. Using only sleek, machine-generated materials can suck the love and personality out of our experiences.

We can shift the narrative by introducing more homemade and handmade items into the mix. Even just a few things here and there will help to turn the tide. We can honor handmade things in the way we talk about them with our kids and call attention to the humanity behind them. Signs of creative labor are beautiful. Stitches, nail holes, and pen strokes come out of the shadows to speak to us of human skill and time. If the highest goal we have is to convey our love to the children we engage with—in school, in church, in our homes—we need to realize that a slightly shabby item made by hand is usually superior to the shiny purchased version.

When we can't make or do something ourselves, another way to honor human creativity is to hire local artisans and makers, especially those who use slow, traditional processes. My family certainly cannot afford to always buy bread at the farmers' market, much less buy handmade clothes or furniture. But as we are able, we find that going to the extra expense slows our rapid accumulation of things, helps our kids respect human craftsmanship, and supports people who are choosing to exercise the creative option.

Commitment two: Find your forte and help kids find theirs. I have found it highly satisfying to carve out small niches where I don't need to be a buyer. I love to consider the question, "Could I do this myself?" before I hire something out or buy it. There are plenty of things I can't do—I learned the hard way that hanging wallpaper is not my forte! The creative option is not always the right option. (That's why I've presented it as an option and not an all-or-nothing tradeoff.) But there should also be times when you have the skills—or could learn them—to create instead of consume. As our children see us exercising skills and talents, it can inspire them to step into creative endeavors themselves.

Most kids start life with a natural confidence in their ability to make and do. "Let me try it!" and "Look what I made!" are healthy expressions of pride that we often hear from little ones. To protect that instinct and revive it in young people who have already lost a bit of their energy and confidence for contributing, we can commit to letting them experiment with things like cooking, yard work, artistic projects, and home maintenance.

If we give kids opportunities to experiment with a variety of creative endeavors, including ones that aren't necessarily arts and crafts related, we can help them find a forte. My parents let my little brother paint a giant whale on his bedroom wall when he was four, and now he is a professional artist! You might not want to start with something as ambitious. But the more freedom you give, the better.

Everyone has something they can contribute to make the world more beautiful. Maybe it's telling jokes. Maybe it is looking after younger siblings, or greeting people at church, or organizing the pantry. There are so many places kids can plug into the fabric of daily life, and doing so helps them to feel capable and happy to contribute. As kids experiment, maybe a single forte expands to two or three—or just remains a signature niche. The important thing is to help them find a way to contribute, and to tap into other people who have found theirs.

Commitment three: Restore the chain for passing on skills. I thought it was the greatest privilege when I was around thirteen years old to watch my grandmother make her famous chocolate sauce topping for ice cream. This was the ultimate secret sauce—no recipe, no equivalent in any cookbooks. Grandmama made it from memory, adjusting proportions by taste and feel. I became her chocolate sauce apprentice one summer on a family beach trip, and by the time Grandmama passed away, I had her method stowed forever in my memory banks. I imagine you had similar experiences growing up. But what about our kids? Is the next generation looped into that chain?

The young man I've already quoted several times doesn't think so: "We have absolutely no institutional sources for acquiring wisdom available for us," he says. Perhaps he overstates the problem, but I think what he means is that many of the relationships as well as formal programs that allowed kids to observe their elders and to practice and hone skills have disappeared. That process, too, has been turned into a consumer experience—simply pull up a YouTube video and get quick advice from a stranger. (And if that isn't boiled down enough, you can use the under-four-minutes filter to acquire "wisdom" in the fewest seconds.)

There could be a whole book written on the perfect storm of factors that broke the chain of passed-down, how-to knowledge, but for our purposes here, we might just note that giving young people more time in the presence of their elders and little apprenticeships (like the chocolate sauce example) can restore the chain for passing creative skills from generation to generation.

Commitment four: Let kids contribute in community settings (outside of the home). "We are no longer embedded in a community to which we contribute." This part of the young man's statement might be the saddest of all. He is right. Where are the places that kids can feel seen and valued in our world of outsourced, professionalized, end user everything?

At the very least, local congregations could be more welcoming to the contributions of children. The church is a body made up of many parts—each person has gifts to contribute (see Romans 12:4-6). But churchgoers cannot mature into this vision if they only see themselves as end users. Much of it has to do with whether we give folks a chance to participate. If your church yard is maintained by a professional crew, for example, it might be a missed opportunity to involve people in a way that helps them live into their identity as contributing members of the body.

Kids also need opportunities to contribute to congregational life, even if what they share feels as small as a few loaves and fish (see John 6:1-14). My nephew recently assisted with the coffee service for our church's morning fellowship. He helped measure the water and brew the coffee (with supervision), then stood by the table to assist. "Would you like sugar?" he asked me with such eagerness that I couldn't refuse.

Children want to contribute to the family of God. So instead of setting up laser tag to entertain kids, why not let them participate in something meaningful? If we wait until adulthood to include them, we shouldn't wonder why they become adults who see church through a consumer lens, with little desire or ability to give of themselves.

HOW TO PRACTICE THE CREATIVE OPTION

I know the suggestions above feel like big shifts that take an entire community's efforts, and that might feel heavy. But each of us can make a difference even on our own. Here are a few practical entry points you can use to give the kids you love access to the creative option:

1. ***Set up an apprenticeship.*** Once we saw that Charlotte was interested in baking as a creative forte, we worked out a little informal apprenticeship with my friend Kendall, a pastry chef. For a few Saturday mornings, Charlotte met her at the restaurant for a behind-the-scenes view of a working kitchen. Kendall passed on recipes, demonstrated methods, and let Charlotte assist. Not only did Charlotte expand her options for creativity, she made a meaningful bond with an adult outside of our family. Apprenticeships where grown-ups pass skills to children don't have to be formal arrangements; they can just be times when kids watch and learn from someone older. And that older someone might be *you*. Let kids watch you! Don't worry if your skills don't feel impressive. If you can't build a treehouse, just make or do something else they can watch:

- Cook your way through your great-aunt's recipes.
- Tune the guitar.
- Propagate African violets.
- Choose paint colors and coordinate fabrics for a room in your house.

   Do *your* job or *your* hobby—whether it's delivering mail, testing pool chemicals, teaching a class, or grooming dogs—and let them look on.

   Full disclosure: letting kids watch requires two effortful things of you. First, you have to endure a child's watchful gaze, potential fidgeting, and incessant questions. This is simply part of the deal. Even animals allow their babies to imprint by watching adults in the species survive. So embrace it!

   Second, the observation approach only works if you yourself have some how-to knowledge worth passing on. You already do—I'm sure of it. But you can also challenge yourself to continue learning new things for the sake of passing them on.

2. *Play with made things rather than purchased ones.* We have a bookshelf full of board games, mostly store-bought. But among our favorites are two handcrafted ones: Henry's "South Carolina-opoly" (made from a recycled box and a $1.25 posterboard) and a storytelling game that the kids came up with where you draw from a hat a character name, settings, and plot twist, and have two minutes to tell a short story. They also create Mad Libs, mazes, crosswords, scavenger hunts, and trivia games for each other. (We go through a lot of paper here!) Often they spend longer making the game than playing it, and that's just fine with me!

3. *Make believe.* Childhood must involve opportunities for kids to creatively repurpose ordinary stuff and use their imaginations to fill in the gaps as they play. Adults need to honor and uphold the creative option by leaving those gaps for little imaginations to fill, *even when you can afford to buy them everything.* If your child says, "Mom! We need a crown because we are playing king and queen," you can either source a store-bought accessory or you can encourage pretending with things already in the house. The second option is the creative one.

4. *Embrace the mess.* I can't mention play and make believe without sharing my sympathy for the toll that extending the creative option takes on your home. I know sometimes it feels easier to say, "Let's just get one at the store" to avoid the mess, but messes are a sign that creative work is underway. Involve your kids in the cleanup as much as possible, and at moments when the living room has been completely torn apart to make the most epic fort ever, or when you discover a giant hole dug in the middle of the lawn to make a tar pit for excavating toy dinosaur bones, just sit back and know that it will be worth it in the long run!

In your practical steps forward, don't feel like you have to dive into the most complex projects right away. Before Charlotte could bake for real, she was making Play-Doh cupcakes. Kid creations won't necessarily substitute for bought goods—especially not early attempts! The important thing is that these experiments form a child's self-concept as a maker rather than an end user. So start small. Teach your little ones to make a birdfeeder out of a pine cone before they take up hammer and nails. Little steps are still valuable ways to opt into creativity.

There will always be false narratives swirling around our kids, telling them that consuming is their ticket to a promised land of leisure and freedom from contributing. Your job is to help them know *by experience* that the real privilege, the real joy, is coming alongside God as co-creators. Help them to hear the Spirit of God beckoning:

> *You have a purpose. You have a gift. Awaken to the value of things that are made—made by me, and made by human hands—and let gratitude wash over you like a refreshing wave.*
>
> *I have called you by name. And I have filled you "with a divine spirit, with ability, intelligence, and knowledge" (Exodus 31:3).*
>
> *Come and add your unique fingerprints, invest your thoughtfulness and energy, so that your labor of love blesses others and reflects my image, through you, to the world.*

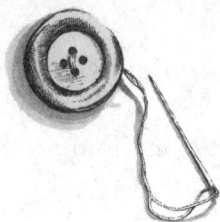

15

Heartfelt Gifts

THE FIRST TIME I JOINED my husband's extended family at their Christmas Eve gathering, I was completely caught off guard by their gift exchange ritual. The best comparison I can think of would be a NASCAR race. Everyone dove into the presents at once, tearing into the gifts as fast as they could. Paper was literally flying through the air. The room was filled with laughter and the sounds of toys whirring. Everyone seemed to be talking over each other. After the presents, without a moment's pause, they pulled down the stockings and tore in, flinging bouncy balls and bubblegum around with glee.

The whole exchange was over in twenty minutes, and the room looked like a stadium after a race—bows and boxes and toys littered the floor. I was only aware of what I had received, clueless about what others had unwrapped or whether they enjoyed the presents that we brought.

On the one hand, I found this way of exchanging gifts exciting and freeing . . . no one had to be patient and wait their turn, or open a gift under the watchful gaze of the giver and think of how to respond on the spot. But on the other hand, I was bewildered. I come from a slow unwrapping tradition. This is probably where I ought to say "different strokes for different folks" so that I don't step on anyone's toes. But I don't actually think all ways of gifting are equal. There are real drawbacks to rushing through the process. It affects how quickly and carelessly we acquire material things, and it speeds past the relational connection at the heart of giving gifts in the first place.

Thankfully, I found that William's family has other rituals that follow up their fast and furious Christmas gift exchange. They nurture heartfelt connections between the giver and the receiver by carefully cataloging who gave what and sending lovely thank-you notes. Over the past twenty years, their Christmas Eve has taken on a gentler pace. As young kids have grown up and parents have become grandparents, just being together feels like the most special gift of the evening.

MINDLESS GIVING AND GETTING

There certainly is not just one right way to go about gifting. But if we are willing, we can review our family traditions in light of the spiritual goals we have for the young people we love.

In our fast-consuming era, the biggest threat to a child's ability to give and receive presents in a heart-to-heart way is the sheer *volume* of stuff kids receive. You might identify with the exasperation of one writer who said, "On behalf of all parents of young children, I offer this holiday plea to all grandparents, aunts, uncles, cousins, teachers, and friends this year: please, for our collective parenting sanity, rein it in with the toys." It's not just that the accumulation is inconvenient for us as parents; it's that the volume of presents depreciates their specialness for kids.

And gift-*giving* can be just as mindless as receiving. One Christmas I actually forgot about a whole bag of presents and didn't find them in the back of my closet until February! I had bought so much for our kids and other family members that I couldn't remember all of it. The next year we made a drastic decision to start giving Charlotte and Henry three thoughtfully chosen gifts each Christmas, plus one present for the whole family to share. There's not a magic number here, but just as less is more on the receiving end, less can be more—more meaningful and more memorable—on the giving end. If the thrill of buying sometimes overwhelms your thoughtfulness, limitations can help. Being more selective actually requires more of your effort, and effort always translates as care.

Heartfelt Gifts

Along with the number of presents, the pace of our exchange deserves a clear-eyed review in light of the spiritual goals we have for our children. Opening quickly usually causes us to disregard the details. It leaves no space to read a card, notice the reaction of the giver or receiver, or make conversation about the item. *Regard* literally means to look twice. And hasty gifting habits barely leave kids time to look once. Even if we spend loads of time in our families procuring and receiving presents, when we divide that time by the number of gifts, each individual present is so quickly bought and so quickly received that it can't be savored.

While there are serious pitfalls that can make giving and getting mindless, God has planted deep within our children's hearts an impulse to give as he gives. It seems to be a primal human instinct—perhaps part of what it means to be made in God's image—that we give objects and services to the ones we love, and that we experience joy when we receive something that was specially selected and presented to us.

Giving gifts is both natural (we were designed for it) and supernatural (we need divine help and empowerment to do it well, to overcome barriers like laziness, selfishness, and hurry). This is true of all the love languages. But gift-giving is the love language that is most degraded by fast-consuming habits because it is essentially material in nature. If kids think of gifts as just stuff to buy, use, and replace at lightning speed, not only will they struggle to respect material things, but they will misunderstand how material things can serve a higher purpose. Let's take some notes from a famous example of gift-giving in Scripture to reawaken us to the sacramental potential of material goods to truly bless both giver and receiver and to convey love.

SLOWING IT DOWN WITH HEARTFELT GIFTS

In one of the most mic-drop moments in the Gospels, a woman named Mary from the village of Bethany gives a gift to Jesus while he is resting at her home. It is just a few short days before his crucifixion, and Mary comes to the dinner table where Jesus and his disciples have just finished a wonderful meal. Ceremoniously, Mary pulls out a jar of pure nard perfume—a product worth a year's salary that wealthy families used in burying their loved ones—and she breaks open the whole jar. Not just a drop, but the entire pound of perfume pours out onto Jesus' feet, filling the room with a powerful and delicious scent. Untying her long hair, Mary then dries Jesus' feet with this extension of her body, the softest and most personal thing she had to offer (John 12:1-8).

It must have been breathtaking to be in that room. Can you imagine the stunned silence? All eyes glued to Mary's hands and the precious jar, wondering what would happen. Some discomfort, perhaps, at the intimacy of the moment when she lowers her face and hair to an inch above the master's feet. And then the fragrance—every nose fills with the scent that brings both delight and memories of solemn burials, a foreshadowing of the bitter days ahead. This woman in their midst had been paying very close attention to the teacher's words. And she chooses a present for Jesus that conveys all of her understanding, her love, and her worship.

But someone in the room thought her gift was careless. Judas, the betrayer, speaks up to criticize Mary's expensive outpouring as a wasteful display. "Leave her alone," Jesus warns Judas. "She has carefully guarded herself and her resources for the sake of honoring my death" (John 12:7, my paraphrase).

This is not a story of careless gift-giving. It's an extravagantly generous, extravagantly selfless, and yet remarkably restrained and precisely timed gift. Full of meaning, full of heart.

The love language of gifts isn't anti-material, nor is it anti-expense. On the contrary, Mary's outpouring and Jesus' response show us that material goods are capable of conveying deep care. But in order for that to happen, the process must involve something *more* than matter and more than money. The episode holds several clues for us about how to help our kids learn the language of loving through presents—honoring both the outward form and the heartfelt intent of a material gift. Even onlookers can be blessed by gifting when it is enriched in this way.

There are many layers of meaning in this story of anointing, but for our purposes here, let's take a look at a few guiding principles we can distill for helping children step into heartfelt gifts.

Limit the number. One heirloom pocket knife passed from grandad to grandson is more significant in the long run than a whole shelf of toys from Target. The principle of restraint will help both the giver and the receiver savor the present.

This is important for families who have fewer resources, but also for families with more. For those with less, slowing down the experience extends the impact of a single gift. It allows the whole group to join in the joy of the one who receives, so that the gift's blessing is multiplied. In households where gifts are more frequent, slowing down the experience and limiting the number of gifts helps children to be less entitled—less conditioned to expect gifts as their due—and more attuned to the gesture as an act of love.

For those who are concerned that occasions like Christmas will feel anticlimactic with so few gifts, see if you can think of other ways to enhance the celebration—singing, for instance. Maybe someone can play an instrument, too. Go caroling to your neighbors' homes. Invite someone from outside the family to join you for some of the day's festivities. Showing our love with gifts is wonderful, but it isn't the only language we have to express our care, and kids thrive when we use a broad range of expressions.

Be extravagant. You might be surprised to find me cheerleading for extravagant gifts a few pages after encouraging you to cultivate simple tastes. I do not mean to suggest that we should teach kids to be more extravagant toward themselves, but more extravagant toward others.

The freedom to pour oneself into a gift with no thought of what it costs (time, money, effort) is actually a sign of simplicity. I don't want my kids to be so attached to their possessions that they can't part with them. Being generous with others to the point of extravagance aligns us with the heart of God. "Observe how Christ loved us," Paul wrote to the Ephesians. "His love was not cautious but extravagant. He didn't love in order to get something from us but to give everything of himself to us. Love like that" (Ephesians 5:2 MSG).

Extravagant generosity doesn't require more money, but it does mean giving sacrificially from whatever you have—time, energy, creativity. A birthday card made by a child, even if it's sticky with glue and missing capital letters, is more extravagant, more *personally* costly on the child's part, than a sleek store-bought card they buy with mom's money. Extravagant gifts can be homemade or purchased, tiny or grand, symbolic or practical. But in some way, the giver of a heartfelt gift puts something of herself into it.

Set the tempo for savoring. Rarely do we dive in the moment a box or bag is handed to us. We wait for the birthday song, or we place gifts under the tree until Christmas morning. At a baby shower we pass around the tiny clothes and soft items for collective oohing and ahhing as a way to share in the excitement. These are all beautiful rituals that provide time for deep regard. Boundaries create time and space for kids to look twice and to see beneath the surface, like Jesus did. He understood the meaning of Mary's perfume gift. He saw her heart. He saw *her*.

HOW TO PRACTICE HEARTFELT GIFTS

Nurturing gracious givers and gracious receivers takes a tough skin. People do not like to have their traditions challenged. And there are so many unique individuals involved in our kids' lives, each with their own ways of gifting. Nevertheless, we have found ways to slow things down.

1. Homemade gifts. Every year for Christmas William writes me a song (well, a rap; it's pretty hilarious). Since kids don't often have money, homemade gifts like songs and crafts are wonderful ways for children to participate on the giving end and not just on the receiving end. Some perennial favorites at our house include: coupon books (for things like doing someone's chores for them or giving a back rub), jewelry made from beads or shells, homemade activity sheets and scavenger hunts, artwork, baked goods, and personalized stationery. A friend told me that homemade gifts might sound unrealistic to families who are less artsy. She has a great point. Creativity comes in many forms. Revisit the chapter on the creative option for tips on helping your child find a niche even if they aren't especially crafty. The real point of homemade gifts isn't about the quality of the end product, but rather pouring one's heart into something for someone else's sake.

2. ***Savor wrapping and unwrapping.*** I have no idea when it first dawned on humankind to wrap a gift. There's nothing holy or sacrosanct about hiding or covering the gift so that it can be opened. But I like the way that thinking through the presentation reflects the giver's thoughtfulness, and I like the way that unwrapping creates space for the receiver to savor every part of the experience. My husband's grandmother remembers getting presents in bespoke boxes and hand-decorated tissue paper in the days before store-bought gift wrap. With a little effort, we can reclaim wrapping as a gift in itself, or at least take time on the receiving end to savor the care that goes into presentation. My sister Catherine does this with her little girls by decorating their own wrapping paper each Christmas. You could try Catherine's method (stencils and paints on butcher paper), or have your kids make the tags, collect and reuse the bows, or decorate plain gift bags with handprints and little love notes. Here's what my sister said about why she does it: "Kids don't have a whole lot of say in what presents get bought, but making the wrapping

gives them ownership in the gift-giving process. It also teaches them intentionality—ironically, by putting care into something that is typically discarded without much thought."

3. **Hold things back for later.** A friend mentioned that she had started putting half of the presents her kids received from out-of-town family members in a closet to stagger over the twelve days of Christmas. She had asked her family to pare down the number of gifts, but it was beyond her control to enforce it. What *was* in her control, however, was *when* the kids opened them—and whether they kept them or regifted them. If you have a similar situation, work within your circumstances to slow it down as much as you can.

4. **Take turns.** Watching and caring about what *other* people receive is an important step in growing out of self-centeredness. For a group to wait and delight in the happiness of both giver and receiver, there needs to be some order to the festivities. My family's tradition is to unwrap gifts one at a time in age order, starting with the youngest in the room. (If you think you have too many gifts to take turns within a reasonable amount of time, you might have too many gifts.) When you are the host, you can say how the group will take turns opening presents. But if you are a guest at someone else's home, just be aware that people can be easily offended if you try to shift their traditions. You can still suggest a rhythm and see if they warm to your idea, but be a gracious participant even if they don't.

5. **Follow up.** A time for show and tell after the gifting is done can help your kids remember and appreciate what they got and help everyone take delight in each other's gifts. (Adults, show and tell your gifts to model how it's done.) "I got a scarf from Grandma and a book from my cousins." A few minutes is all it takes to let each person recap for the group what they might have missed seeing opened. And find a way to say thank you. Kids can draw

a thank-you card, write a note, or give a verbal thank-you to savor the connection as they enjoy the gift.

When gift exchanges fall short of heartfelt intentions—and they will!—you can follow up with a gentle discussion about what was missing and how it could be better. Even negative experiences can be fruitful learning spaces. Without being overly critical, simply ask your child questions like, "Did you get to see if Grandmom liked her present? Aw man, well maybe next time we can ask her to wait and open it when we are near her." These honest conversations between adults and kids are surprisingly powerful ways to help young people form healthy values. Reflective discussions and family practices for savoring gifts may feel like very small acts of resistance in a fast-consuming world, but every step to slow it down expands your child's capacity for loving others by giving—and for living in closer communion with the Giver of all.

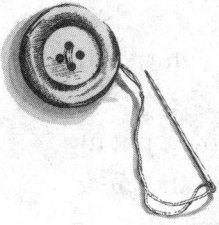

16

Revival Skills

BY THE AGE OF THREE, our daughter Charlotte could draw better than most adults. I'm not exaggerating. People would stop in their tracks to watch her, slightly incredulous that this little child could not only render with such skill, but that she could imagine the interesting and intricate designs she created.

Despite this amazing talent, little Charlotte was often frustrated that her hand would not deliver the vision she had in her head. She was a perfectionist from birth. We never pressured her to achieve any-thing artistically. She had her own standards, and when her artwork didn't look the way she wanted it, she would ball up her drawing and cast the paper away in disgust. After any art session, you could find her surrounded by a pile of rejects on the floor.

We tried everything to coax Charlotte to be gentler on herself. We praised the cast-off art—it was actually good!—but that didn't help. It didn't match the image in her brain, and we weren't going to talk her out of it.

We tried appealing to her sense of right and wrong by telling her not to waste the paper, but that didn't help either.

We tried getting her to use a pencil so she could erase what she wasn't happy with, but she only liked crayons and pens.

Finally, I found an angle that worked. One day as Charlotte flung aside a piece of paper she had barely made any marks on, I rescued it from the trash pile and told her, "Hey, want to see a neat trick? It's fun to see if you can save a mess-up and turn it into art."

I took her abandoned drawing and flipped it upside down, put my pencil against the line she had started, and continued it up and out to form a tree. Charlotte was drawn in by the challenge. From then on, our family's consumption of craft paper was drastically reduced. And I think it helped sustain Charlotte's interest in drawing. (The beautiful images in this book are from her pen!)

I brought up this memory the other day, and Charlotte laughed and said, "That was the best thing you ever taught me." She was exaggerating, of course, but it's funny to think that such a small practice totally transformed her outlook on something she considered flawed beyond use.

ACCEPTING OBSOLESCENCE

For most of us, throwing things away is an unexamined part of life. It's muscle memory. And that goes for more than what we fit in our garbage cans. For the past hundred years, economic growth has fed on a business strategy known as planned obsolescence. Instead of producing something durable and high quality, businesses intentionally shorten the shelf life of their products to accelerate the replacement cycle and drive up profits.

Peter Mommsen, editor at *Plough* magazine, writes about the nineteenth-century shift from a business ethic that took pride in making "products that were durable and repairable," like Singer sewing machines and Ford's Model T, to the sales-growth strategy pioneered by General Motors "to hasten obsolescence." Downgrading quality and updating styles every year encouraged customers to replace rather than repair. Now, Mommsen observes, "the quickening replacement cycle for things we buy has become so embedded in daily life that it seems part of the natural order of things."

Such a strategy might win our dollars if we have any of these weak spots:

- attraction to trends
- susceptibility to bargain euphoria (this one really gets me!)

- underdeveloped skills for maintenance
- an aversion to the effort of upkeep

Kids pick up on the values that underlie their families' consumer habits. Recently, companies have leveraged social media to draw in kids as consumers and to push a faster and faster cycle of trend changes. Social media creates a buzz around new products and, in quick order, creates a completely new and different trend so that clothes, products, and technologies will be discarded and replaced in rapid succession. "The concept of marketing to kids isn't new," observes the advocacy group Common Sense Media, "but social media amplifies marketing's reach and personalization, which makes it more impactful and often more toxic to our kids. . . . They take advantage of young viewers' natural insecurities and their desires for connection and belonging."

Of course none of us wants our children to grow up thinking that they need to have the newest stuff to find belonging and connection. How can we counter the "newer is better" mantra and the "buy, throw away, replace" ethic that children encounter in the marketplace? And how might we help kids see the possibilities in what they already have? I think the answer lies in giving kids the vision and skills to save things they thought were worthless.

SLOWING IT DOWN WITH REVIVAL SKILLS

A few years ago we bought a one-hundred-year-old property next door to my parents that I'm pretty sure would have scared most buyers! It was a *major* fixer-upper. But we were brave—and we were desperate for something we could afford. The house had loads of character—cool original details, but also wonky stairs, quirky rooms, and a few holes in the ceilings. Despite its imperfections, it's my dream house. But it needed a lot of TLC to bring it back to life.

As we have worked on reviving this home, God has worked on reviving us. (If you have lived through a renovation, you know what I'm talking about!) Renovating an older home—or just living in a place that isn't new, for that matter—is a little act of rebellion against the replacement cycle. It comes with many opportunities to make do and be resourceful. And it teaches you to see potential.

Our old house didn't have a bathroom on the ground floor and didn't have anywhere to put the laundry machines. These were not standard features when the house was built in 1924. We lived with things the way that they were for a while. And then when we could afford to do some renovating, we had to get creative in order to fit a new bathroom and laundry room within the confines of the existing space. We also salvaged the wood flooring that we pulled out in the new laundry space and used it to patch holes in the floor elsewhere around the house. These are just a few examples of the challenges and lessons of renovating.

By growing up in a not-new home, my children have developed a broader view of what makes something beautiful. They know how to spot the craftsmanship of buildings, even when they're in a state of disrepair. They value history; they know that older things can be just as special, and that signs of wear are often signs of love.

In the process of reviving our home, I believe we've taught our kids to bear with some discomfort. We have involved them in forms of maintenance and repair that, hopefully, will help them resist the replacement-cycle trap as they grow up. They have scraped wallpaper and swung sledgehammers. (Video evidence exists!) They have helped to dig out invasive bamboo and replace a damaged roof on a play-house. We may have overdone it a bit—I think the early days of living here without heat and air was less of a fun adventure and more of a trial by fire! But at least our kids don't think that climate-controlled interiors are absolutely necessary for survival.

Making do, salvaging, bearing with discomfort, seeing through the outer condition to the essential worth of a thing, and putting effort into repair—these are all *revival skills*. They translate into every arena of life. And children who learn revival skills have a huge leg up when it comes to avoiding fast consuming. They behold the world with the eyes of a revivalist and have practical abilities to live that way.

At the root of the word *revival* is the word for life (-*viv*-). In any given context, revival has to do with bringing something back to life or back to strength. You can revive someone who has fainted, and you can revive a stagnant career. You can revive a language on the brink of extinction, or revive wilting plants with fresh water. In the world of art, revival means creating something new in the style of something old, thereby giving new life to a dying aesthetic, a musical style, or an artistic method. Neighborhoods and cities can experience revival. And when a wave of renewed interest and commitment to Jesus sweeps through a community, we call it a revival.

Of all the antidotes to fast consuming that we have covered, revival skills might be the most important, because they don't just shape the way kids buy stuff; they shape their outlook on everything and everyone as savable. This is God's outlook, after all. God is aware of every crack in our character. He sees every unwholesome thought and every off-kilter perspective in us. He knows we have foundation issues under the surface, where selfish desires still push and pull us. But even in that state, he doesn't see us as worthless. He sees us as worth saving.

A throwaway mindset diminishes a child's capacity to see as God sees and to love as God loves. But a revival mindset instills wisdom for a kingdom life. As our children develop the desire and skill to mend and restore material things, we hope that they will want to practice that same kind of care toward everything and everyone that God has made. For example, we hope they will have:

- *An eye for value.* Instead of seeing only two possibilities—new and perfect or old and worthless—a revival mindset sees a third possibility: worth saving.

- *Tenderness.* Feeling sad about destruction and disposal isn't being overly sentimental. It's being awake to the value of made things. A revival mindset gives kids space to lament loss. Lost resources, lost relationships, and lost and lonely people break God's heart, and they should break ours, too.

- **Eagerness to repair,** especially when they have caused the damage. A revival mindset trains kids to look for ways to make things better. This might look like reconciling after an argument, cleaning up a mess, attempting to restore a bird's nest that got knocked down, or a hundred other revival-inspired acts of love.

- ***Humility and a collaborative spirit.*** If you can't fix something yourself, ask for help, or employ fix-it folks. A revival mindset teaches kids to seek out people with the skills to reclaim, restore, and redeem all sorts of things, to learn from them, and to collaborate with them.

I think these qualities come naturally to children. But they also can be nurtured or crushed by family habits. For example, if your child has a stuffed animal or blanket that they care about, what happens as it gets faded and worn over time? A little act like sewing up a hole in a blanket can help a young child see that old things are worth fixing, and that fixed things are still lovely. Sometimes revived items are even *more* special.

HOW TO PRACTICE REVIVAL SKILLS

Showing Charlotte how to salvage her messed-up drawing and turn it into something useful was a little victory. But it would be dishonest for me to pretend that we have mastered revival! Living completely waste-free feels like an impossible goal, but small acts that circumvent the rapid replacement cycle feel doable. As we have practiced small acts of repair and restoration, our children's revival skills have grown.

1. Mending. I learned from a veteran preschool teacher that stitching is a wonderful activity for little hands. Henry has mended many of his stuffed animals. Henry's stitching is not particularly neat, but at least it's functional. Another form of mending we have embraced is book repair. We've had a few books rebound that are special to our family, and last Christmas Charlotte surprised me by recovering my Bible. With a leather scrap from the hobby store, special glue, and some patterned paper for the inside covers, she brought the worn-out Bible back to life! If you have books at your house that are falling apart, try making homemade covers, or take a field trip to meet an expert in book repair.

2. ***Repurposing.*** My brother is a master at repurposing. He keeps a container of recyclables—the "bits and bobs" box—full of items that would have gone in the trash. Sometimes the bits and bobs find new life as parts for kids' art projects, and other times they get pulled out as toy repair parts, drawer organizers, and other such reincarnations. Before throwing things away, we can ask our children, "What could we do with this?" and see what ideas they have.

3. ***Normalizing patina.*** I'm the daughter of a sculptor, so I love the word *patina* (puh-TEE-nuh). It's the color change that happens over time to bronze and other metals through weather exposure. I like to use the word *patina* widely—like the way some people use the word *character*—to mean signs of age and wear that add beauty and interest. For example, our plates and cups have tiny cracks and chips—patina! Our living room furniture is well made and cozy, but also a bit faded—patina! Surrounding kids with newness diminishes their ability to appreciate patina. City kids might have an advantage over suburban kids in this respect. Suburbia is often so brand new, so manicured, so shiny and perfect that children who spend all their time there have no taste for patina. Kids can see plenty of new stuff in a city, too, but they will also see traces of the past: historic buildings in various stages of aging or repair, bridges under restoration, preserved monuments, and repurposed structures. To grow your child's appreciation for patina try visiting an older part of town or take a field trip to an antiques shop.

4. *Saying sorry.* Relationships require maintenance and repair too. A heartfelt apology, a hug, a note–these are powerful tools for revival when feelings are bruised. As kids age up, they will learn that harsh words and irresponsible decisions cause rifts. Teaching them to address and repair little cracks is essential for learning to handle conflict in a healthy way instead of abandoning relationships.

To savor is, in a sense, to *save*. To treasure and enjoy something rather than quickly discarding it. Our efforts to mend and restore may not always succeed, but practicing revival skills means doing what we can to bring something back to life or back to strength so we can savor it. Joining God as partners in mending is resurrection work! In its own small way, our use of things bears the testimony of salvation.

PART 5

Slow Growing Up

TODAY IS HENRY'S FIFTH GRADE DAY CELEBRATION. The festivities include games and class parties, followed by a parade where the fifth graders take a victory lap through the elementary school hallways and weave their way around to the middle school to ceremonially become sixth graders.

On the drive there, Henry was eating a bagel and I was enjoying the ride as a chance to ask him questions and listen to him talk. I always find the conversation flows well with my son when just the two of us are in the car together, and I love hearing my children's perspectives on current events (the big global kind, and the day-in-the-life of an eleven-year-old kind). Sometimes they get annoyed with my more probing questions, but other times they seem to enjoy a chance to share their ideas.

This morning's conversation gave me an inside peek at Henry's views on himself and on childhood.

"Can I ask you your opinion on something?" I began. "I have been wondering about it, and want to hear some children's ideas."

"Do I still count as *children*?" he said, enunciating the word *children* with extra formality. There was a hint of laughter in his voice, but I also detected some genuine uncertainty, given that this was his last day of elementary school.

"Hmmm, I think so," I said, "but let me check. . . . You are not an adult, are you?" We both laughed.

And then he asked about his big sister, "What about Charlotte? Are fifteen-year-olds *children*?"

"Yes, Charlotte is a teenage child, but she is still a child," I reassured him. I was also reassuring myself.

It gave my heart a sudden twinge of anguish to imagine either of my children not being children anymore. This is a bittersweet part of loving young people—they grow up. Eventually this chapter of their lives will be fulfilled, the page will turn, and the next chapter will begin. Sometimes it feels like if I blink, that page will turn before I'm ready.

I know well the sensation of wanting to freeze-frame childhood. The impulse to want to slow it down comes from a good desire to savor the time because we realize that it really doesn't last forever. But growth is beautiful. Jesus the incarnate Son grew up. Becoming an adult didn't corrupt him or drain him of holiness. He didn't lose his imagination or joy by aging. On the contrary, his wisdom, character, grace, and relationships deepened as he grew (see Luke 2:52). It is God's design that humans begin as babies and grow up into adults. There mustn't be a Peter Pan syndrome affecting a Christian view of childhood. Childhood is neither more sacred nor less sacred than adulthood. Every age and stage of human life has equal potential to be lived "to the full"—in harmony with God, others, and the world (John 10:10 NIV).

Having admitted that I know the sensation of wanting to freeze-frame childhood, I should also confess that I know the sensation of wanting to speed up childhood when it feels tough. Isn't it funny that we can hold both of these distorted wishes in our minds—to want to keep children little forever and also to want them to be as mature and self-reliant and accomplished as adults?

Henry's question about whether he was still a child made me laugh, but it actually captures the way many of us feel—unsure about when childhood stops. Is it when they turn double digits? When they drive? When they graduate from high school? Or when their frontal cortex is fully formed? People also seem very unsure about how to help young people take on more mature types of activities and pursuits at a pace that still leaves room for them to be kids.

I am not here to make any claims on the exact boundaries of childhood in terms of years and months. No matter how you measure it, today's young people are not getting the chance to experience childhood "to the full."

At this point in the book, we have looked at four forms of hurry that contribute to the problem. A final form of hurry we must address is rushing kids to grow up too quickly.

Just as we have to stop regretting the progression of childhood and fretting over its brevity in order to sink into and savor it, we also have to beware of taking it for granted or being so focused on clearing milestones that we hurry past formative and beautiful experiences. It's easy to feel exasperated with a child for not having the maturity of an adult. It can try your patience to the point that you think, "Lord, can we just skip *this* part?" Whether it's potty training or middle school mood swings, sitting through a first-year violin concert or sitting in the principal's office to discuss a child's behavior, some parts of childhood feel more like surviving than savoring.

And if I am completely honest, some parts can be boring. Spending quality time with a young child takes so much energy and effort, and some of the responsibilities are as dull as a carpool line (and I think a carpool line might be the universally accepted symbol for *dull*). I can remember playtimes with the kids when they were in preschool. The minutes crawled by as we acted out the same little scenes over and over again with trains or dolls or stuffed animals. Sometimes I would escape to the bathroom or check the weather just for a change in pace! Or I would work something into the plot of our pretending that gave me a rest: "Okay, now pretend like the mommy tiger is sick and needs to lie down here while the baby tiger keeps playing."

There are moments where we might wish (subconsciously) that kids would hurry and grow up. To have the thought is normal. To *act* on it—to discourage a young child from playing in an age-appropriate way or repeatedly asking questions or trying something over and over again—is to actively rush them out of the green pastures where their young souls need to linger.

Another way to spin the top on childhood is to get so focused on securing a child's *future* that her present needs get skipped over. A head start on academics, sports, and other goals is fine unless it turns childhood into a tiny career-building exercise—rushing kids into achievements, commitments, and public exposures so that they don't have the downtime and the anonymity they need to be a kid.

We do not need to prolong, pause, or freeze childhood in order to savor it, but we do need to stop rushing kids toward adulthood. I believe with the Lord's help we can give kids the chance to enjoy childhood "to the full."

This section of *Savoring Childhood* is about giving children access to relationships and experiences that shape a healthy outlook on the world, themselves, and God. So many experiences contribute something essential to that formation, and a few of my favorites—like creative projects and imaginative play—show up in almost every chapter of this book!

Is God good? How do I hear God and talk to God? Where do I belong? What makes me who I am? What is true and trustworthy? These are questions kids are exploring in childhood—not just through Sunday school lessons and catechisms. (Though, as a teacher I certainly believe those are excellent tools. Formal teaching was a part of Jesus' boyhood, and our kids need it too.) But our children need *more* than just formalized instruction to truly know God. They need personal encounters with God's goodness and nearness. And these lessons must not be rushed.

Slowing down the growing-up process puts kids back in touch with all sorts of delightful experiences, including the most important form of savoring—to "taste and see that the LORD is good" (Psalm 34:8). The next three chapters take us deeper into essential building blocks for a wholesome childhood:

- "Animal Friends" connects young people to the natural world, which draws them into a relationship with God as his beloved children and coworkers in creation.

- "Reading Down" is about sharing stories that root children in truth and belonging.

- "Counterpoints" provides the missing ingredients kids need to connect with God. As we restore balance to our children's lives, they learn to discern what their souls need.

"You are only a child once," the saying goes. And in a sense, this is true. Some of you may feel that you grew up too quickly to soak in some of childhood's essential nutrients. But that doesn't mean that all is lost. The invitations of this book are also for you—because all of us, no matter how old we are, are called by Jesus to "become like children" (Matthew 18:3).

One of Jesus' students, a man named Nicodemus, asked him the question we all want to know: "How can anyone be born after having grown old?" (John 3:4). We can't actually go back to kindergarten or relive middle school. (Let's thank God for that!) Jesus explained to him that the second birth isn't a physical process. It's a spiritual one. It is the work of God in our lives that comes not by a physical regression of any kind, but by being humble enough to rethink things. If you have a childlike eagerness to learn and imitate, if you are willing to take all that you believe, want, and do by habit, and offer every bit of it to the Holy Spirit for revision, God will transform you. This is how a person of any age can be born again and "renewed day by day" (2 Corinthians 4:16).

The life lessons and encounters of a slow and spacious childhood lay foundations for an eternity of loving communion with God. You, too, are welcome to meet him here.

17

Animal Friends

AFTER MY MOM READ ME *The Secret Garden* when I was about five or six, I was convinced that the robins in my yard could talk to me and unveil secrets. I longed for them to lead me to an opening in the fence of my backyard that would reveal an undiscovered "bit of earth" to call my own.

I didn't grow up on a farm or in a particularly wildlife-rich environment. But there were critters, nonetheless. And the ones that lived in my backyard appeared to my childhood sensibilities to be both friends and protectees. I was eager to have a role in God's caretaking mission on earth.

One spring, when the massive nest of caterpillar larvae in our double black cherry tree suddenly erupted with thousands of baby caterpillars, I felt these hatchlings needed for me to make them an orphanage out of sticks and to bring them food and water.

I have loved seeing my kids express that same instinct to befriend and protect God's world. For instance, Henry has discovered that every April, a colony of ground-nesting bees emerges from the soil in one part of our yard. Eager to befriend them, he watched their movements with a close eye and tried bringing them offerings of flowers and food. When he realized that this variety of bee does not sting, he decided to catch some of them, observe them up close, and carry them around with him for a bit before releasing them. One that was overhandled died, and Henry was so sorry about it that he built a tiny burial mound for the deceased bee and gave it a proper funeral with flowers, hymns, and a cross. In his childlike way, he was participating in what he felt to be good work: collaboration with the God who cares for every sparrow—and surely every mason bee too.

LOSING TOUCH WITH THE CREATOR

"God *wants* to be seen," the medieval author Julian of Norwich proclaims, "and he wishes to be sought, and he wishes to be expected, and he wishes to be trusted."

Make no mistake, though the Almighty is invisible, he has filled the cosmos with his fingerprints and activity so that all of us can, as Paul wrote, "fumble about for him and find him—though indeed he is not far from each one of us. For 'In him we live and move and have our being'" (Acts 17:27-28). God is hiding in plain sight, so to speak. And he means for the finding to be delightful for us.

God is longing to show himself to us as clearly and beautifully as our limited human senses can possibly take him in. But for all of us, young and old, learning to see him and trust him is a bit of a process, which is why having a full and unrushed time to be a kid and experience childhood's fertile spaces for spiritual growth is so essential. Chief among those spaces where God reveals himself to little ones and develops the bonds of attraction and trust is the realm of nature. The fact that nature is an excellent starting place for children to connect with God fits with the pattern of how God first introduced himself to humanity—as the Creator of a beautiful world. Every created thing is radiant with his touch and ready to speak something to children about the Maker.

But of all the generations of humans since the very beginning, the current generation might be the most disconnected from God's self-revelation in nature. We have already discussed some of the reasons why. Kids with busy schedules and media-saturated attention aren't likely to sit bored by a window where they might spy a little chipmunk madly dashing across the driveway to squeeze under the shed. Kids conditioned by instant gratification aren't likely to patiently observe their natural surroundings, expectantly waiting for subtle signs of God's presence to emerge. And other shifts in modern life have separated children from the land and its animals.

The result is that all of us, grown-ups and young people, have lost a natural pathway to knowing God and to knowing ourselves as his children and his partners in caring for creation. Losing that touchpoint not only shrinks our view of God; it inflates our view of problems. The pall of despair that covers modern life is based on a narrow and distorted view of reality. True, there are significant things that deserve our concern—environmental issues, justice issues, and so on—and God wants to mobilize us as his partners in addressing these needs. But most of what we worry about and most of our children's anxieties and fears are the result of being overexposed to ugliness and underexposed to majesty. Instead of rushing children into adult awareness of the world's problems—or the opposite extreme, rushing to shield them from reality—we need to reconnect them with nature, where they can encounter God in the midst of gentle introductions to both hardship and beauty.

SLOWING IT DOWN WITH ANIMAL FRIENDS

Before God made humans—and this sequence holds up whether you take the Genesis timeline as literal or metaphorical, and even if you look outside Scripture to geological evidence—God made other animals first. All sorts. And he calls his animal creatures good—not that they have a morality, so to speak, but their existence brings something delightful into the broader scheme of all that he has made. When a child has time to observe, touch, appreciate, and wonder about animals, the inherent goodness of creation is self-evident. Delighting in animals brings kids into agreement with what God calls good. And it invites them to step into the caregiving role that God originally intended for humans to have with the world and its inhabitants.

Paying attention to God's creation is like a second scripture—a primary form of God's self-revelation that children at all stages need time to soak in just as much as they need time to soak in the Bible and other forms of revelation.

From Charlotte's and Henry's earliest days, we pointed enthusiastically to animals in the yard or in storybook illustrations. We made animal sounds and taught them to identify creatures by name. We sang songs about animals and thanked God for the animals in our prayers.

Taking time to notice and delight in creatures is something our family has nurtured as an essential part of childhood precisely because friendship with animals is such a natural basis for friendship with God. I drew the title for this chapter from a favorite book at our house, *Our Animal Friends at Maple Hill Farm*. The simply illustrated paperback gives a humorous who's who of geese, horses, sheep, cats, dogs, and chickens on a farm, sketching out their daily lives in such a delightful way that readers can't help but be drawn into appreciation for the Creator. My children's firsthand experience of the animal kingdom is through city critters, not livestock, but they think of the creatures in our neighborhood as their friends.

In observing and interacting with animals, kids encounter a whole host of important life lessons. Let's look at a few that we wouldn't want to rush past:

An antidote to anxiety. "I tell you, do not worry about your life," Jesus told his followers (Luke 12:22). He doesn't just command it; he follows up with a practical strategy for letting go of worry. "Consider the ravens," he continues; "they neither sow nor reap, they have neither storehouse nor barn; and yet God feeds them" (Luke 12:24). Jesus understood that nature draws us up to a God's-eye view of things that supersedes our fears and worries. So kids need time and space to simply look at creatures—in the yard, at the zoo, in books, under microscopes, at the beach, and in the park. Even without making a big theological lesson out of it, simply observing animals and paying attention to their features and behaviors is a mini lesson on God's provision and care for everything he has made, including us. Helping children to consider animals ought to be our first line of defense against anxiety, because Jesus commends it.

Wisdom about life and death. The animal kingdom has other lessons too. We might scoff at the old-fashioned "birds and the bees" way to broach a certain subject, but I will tell you that when human reproduction came up for discussion with our son, his nonchalant response was, "Oh yeah, you mean mating." Of course, there's more to it than that, but it was wonderful that his familiarity with the animal kingdom helped to form his understanding of reproduction as a good, natural part of God's design.

And don't forget another natural process—death. In generations past, death was much more frequent and familiar to young children. Certainly we don't want to go back to a more pervasive presence of suffering and death. But since death is still an unavoidable fact of life, it's good for children to have some introductions that help them understand that life is fragile, that grief is okay, that God is near.

Without opportunities to process death, children can find it hard to grasp the value and preciousness of life. (And that missing value lies at the root of so many tragic forms of violence and contempt in modern culture.) A very small way to work toward helping kids see human life as sacred is to involve them in the lives of animals. The life cycles of pets and wild animals can be small doorways that open up healthy conversation so that death is not an abstract or surreal concept for young people. Let your kids spend an entire afternoon at the beach rescuing stranded starfish. Let them bury the guinea pig and paint a rock for the headstone. Let them place flowers on the miniature burial mound of a mason bee and construct a cross out of sticks and hot glue.

I'm not trying to be morbid, but the well-being of our communities depends, to a degree, on the emotional health of each child. And we can nurture that development by letting kids experience a healthy grief over death and a healthy respect for the miracle of life. Animal friendships help us take little steps into this complex topic.

Doorways to prayer. When kids experience sadness or concern about their animal friends, or joy and delight, those emotions are excellent fodder for conversation with the Lord. Feelings can be a good beginning place for prayer, as the psalms show us.

Oh, the heartfelt prayers our children offered for a sick, stranded kitten, Cookie, who was later renamed Agatha June (perhaps the name change reflects her upward mobility from street kitten to proper inside cat).

Oh, the many expressions of true praise we have witnessed in their "thank you, God" prayers for the animal kingdom broadscale, for dinosaurs (*and* pterosaurs!), for the neighbor's dog, and so on.

My sister's child prayed recently, "God, we thank you for the poor little bird who died. He flew into the window and broke his poor little neck. He was just trying to get some food or something, and he broke his poor little neck. Amen."

Children are learning to pray—to enter that interactive conversation with the Holy One that is the most basic ingredient of real relationship—and encouraging kids to care for creatures and to speak with God about them opens a doorway into prayer.

Partners with God. Not only are animals a sign of God's goodness, a source of important life lessons, and an excellent topic for prayer, they also present children (and all of us) with a realm for collaboration with the Father, Son, and Spirit.

I was encouraged by my parents to practice small, caring acts of protection in the lives of animals. And I felt—even before I had language to communicate it—that this was a way of collaborating with the Creator, of doing my small part to partner with him in his work in the world that he made and that he loves.

Older kids need animal joy too. I would be remiss if I didn't mention that pre-teens and teens are especially needy for ways to give and receive affection, for activities that offer them a slower pace and a break from academic and other pressures, and for opportunities to trade indoor, digital interactions for real, embodied connections with the natural world.

When she was thirteen, I took Charlotte on a trip to Canada where we visited Parc Omega, a 2,200-acre nature preserve outside of Montreal. Charlotte walked around with pygmy deer, fed elk out of her palm, and got up close to bison, boars, and caribou. I saw the delight in her face, and I could sense the refreshment in her spirit.

It takes a little more planning and ingenuity to continue animal friendships as kids get older. But it is important that kids don't associate growing up with growing out of these connections with the natural world. Older kids have the advantage of age and experience, which means you can let them explore nature with less supervision. Letting kids venture out on their own into the realm of plants and animals can set the stage for a powerful encounter with God. And as children age up, they can connect with the mind of the Maker in more ways—through books about zoology, through the biblical psalms that praise the Lord of all creation, through quality nature videos, science courses, and hobbies like collecting shells or shark teeth, and by taking on more responsibility with pets or participating in environmental conservation and care.

HOW TO PRACTICE ANIMAL FRIENDS

Let's look at some practical ways you can create the conditions for your child to make some animal friends or encounter God through the beauty of nature.

1. Involve kids in animal care. Chores like walking the dog or feeding the chickens are great ways to strengthen caregiving impulses, but you don't have to live on a farm or even have pets to include children in taking care of God's creatures. A child can bring leaves to the baby caterpillars in the park or fill the birdbath with water. Acts of care may be instinctive like this, but we can also give young people hints for how to interact. During a recent snowstorm, my mom showed the kids how to put birdseed on the window ledges so the robins, cedar waxwings, and wrens in our yard would have something to eat.

2. *Nature art.* Animals are the perfect subject matter for art projects at every age—from a child's earliest attempts at finger painting all the way up into adulthood. The artist must pay close attention to what she is painting, and in that attentive posture, the glorious intricacies of God's creation come into focus. On the cover of *Our Animal Friends at Maple Hill Farm* are little hand-drawn cameos of each animal friend, displayed in mismatched picture frames like family portraits. We took that cover art as our inspiration for a little art project Henry did in first grade. He drew some of his animal friends from our yard in the style of the book's cover and we framed it for his room. His poster included blue jays, snakes, a worm, two particular squirrels that the kids named Tobias and Jamie, three fish from our pond (now deceased), a hawk, our cat, and a mason bee. Henry did most of the inscribing and all of the drawing himself. The portraits hang proudly in his room to this day—a little connection point to the non-anxious, beautiful creatures he loves.

3. *Storm watching* has always been a favorite way to shift my perspective, and I brought the kids in on it at an early age. (I don't mean storm chasing or anything dangerous! I mean watching at the window as wind blows the tree tops and lightning streaks the sky.) Many children are scared of thunder—and rightly so! The power of nature that we see in the bolt of lightning and hear and feel reverberating through our bodies in the peal that follows is certainly a reminder that we control so little, that we are small and vulnerable. I didn't want my kids to feel overly afraid, but I think there is something good about noticing the intensity of a storm and respecting it as a powerful and majestic force. It's easy

to see why the term *thunderstruck* entered the English vocabulary as a word for feeling bowled over with amazement.

4. ***Make animal-watching a special alternative to a nap for little ones.*** "Would you like to sit on the porch and watch for birds and squirrels instead of a nap today?" If your kids are anything like mine, they will say *yes!* Here's a special opportunity to practice being quiet and still so the little animals will come out of hiding—which will feel like a special treat for kids and will provide tired parents the benefit of some quiet space. Start with short timeframes (five minutes, working up to ten, and finally twenty). Give them something tactile to use in their observation to help them focus. For example, have them make a crayon mark for every animal they see and show you their tally at the end of ten minutes. It is a more advanced form of attentiveness if your child has the capacity to simply sit and watch, but don't be discouraged if it doesn't happen right away. Attentiveness is cultivated and trained, little by little. Learning good animal-attending skills is really training the ability to focus and be present. Simple observation lays the groundwork for *inward* contemplation (reflecting on things in your thoughts) and *upward* contemplation (prayerful attentiveness to the invisible presence and voice of God).

Nature gazing and animal friends aren't just for children. They also help return grown-ups to a non-anxious, trusting, and prayerful communion with the Lord.

I have an almost daily habit of going to our city's park—a little Eden in the heart of downtown. Walking beside the river one day, I saw a great blue heron out of the corner of my eye. The large, lanky bird was standing near some boulders at the bottom of the waterfall, and I felt a strange sensation that something amazing was about to happen. The heron seemed locked in on something. Hungry to see his dinosaur-like predation in action, I walked nearer. I waited and watched. He waited and watched. Suddenly he took a couple of steps, stuck his long neck out impossibly far, and to my amazement, jerked his head back with a brown water snake in his bill, as thick around as a garden hose! As I was marveling at the wild majesty of this display, another surprise: The water snake was trying to choke down a sunfish! The sunfish wriggled in the snake's jaws, and the snake writhed in the heron's beak, and I stood there with my cup running over, amazed and grateful to be privy to such a spectacular showdown. Praise be to God! I couldn't wait to tell the family.

One way we can "become like children" is to keep nurturing our bond with God's world and all his animal friends, no matter how old we are.

18

Reading Down

HENRY AND I WERE READY for our next book together. Even though he no longer needed reading help from mom and dad, we kept up a practice as a way to spend quality time before bed. Our loose pattern was to alternate one book together and one book on his own. Our last two books together—*The Hobbit* and *Black Beauty*—were both my recommendations, so this time I told Henry he should choose.

What a tender surprise to come up to Henry's room and find that he had chosen a little book that I used to read to him when he was very young, *The Runaway Bunny* by Margaret Wise Brown. This is essentially a baby book, a short picture book with one or two lines of text per page.

On the surface the story is simple. It's about a little bunny who tells his mother he is planning to strike out on his own, traveling all over the face of the earth—sailing here and there, climbing a mountain, and so on. Each time Little Bunny announces one of his runaway schemes, Mother Bunny reassures him that no matter where he goes, she will find him and be with him. Eventually Little Bunny decides that all of his grand plans are fine, but what he really wants is to be with her. (I'm crying just writing about it!)

Even though it isn't a book that mentions God, I find it to be a theologically rich story. When Little Bunny says, for example, that he is going to become a bird and fly away, Mother Bunny answers, "If you become a bird and fly away from me, I will be a tree that you come home to." The words stir my imagination with echoes of Psalm 139:

"If I take the wings of the morning and settle at the farthest limits of the sea, even there your hand shall lead me, and your right hand shall hold me fast" (Psalm 139:9).

Henry was becoming a big kid in many ways, but this book was still a connection point between him and his mommy. And I believe it was also a connection point for him with deep truth—the kind that reminds you who you are and what matters most. At any age, the message that nothing can separate you from the One who loves you and that you are deeply desired, pursued, and welcomed is a good word for the soul. Henry might not have been able to articulate why he chose *The Runaway Bunny*. But I knew.

ACCELERATED READING

Accelerated reading, or "reading up," is exposing kids to literature above their current grade level. We do a lot of reading up at our house—to stretch vocabulary skills, introduce imagery and great storylines, and raise important philosophical questions that are part of a child's growing orientation to truth and goodness. But pushing kids to *always* read over their heads spins the top too fast for children to get their bearings.

Treating children like mini adults and overemphasizing academic achievement causes parents and teachers to cut ties with books and stories that are for younger kids (or even for kids their own age who aren't advanced readers). The intention might be to help the child succeed, but that's a version of success based entirely on intellectual development, not the well-being of the child as a whole person—body, mind, and spirit.

"The desperate need today," writes Richard Foster, "is not for a greater number of intelligent people, or gifted people, but for *deep* people." Rushing into adult-paced, adult-themed stories for the sake of intellectual growth zooms past crucial ingredients for depth, but emotional bonding around shared family favorites can instill a sense of belonging and moral values.

In her article "We Need Moral Direction," Gen Z writer Freya India describes the general sense of lostness among her peers: "We rely on all these *experts*–influencers, therapists, dating coaches–to tell us what to do. And the more we turn to them the less we trust ourselves. . . . There's a reason we call it a *moral compass*, and when people abandon it we say they have *lost their way*." While she doesn't directly point to the loss of childhood stories as a reason why young people are grasping for moral direction, India does mention the importance of conveying truth from one generation to the next. "The problem is, when you don't pass moral values onto your children, the world does it for you. It imposes its own values. Values that are ever-changing."

How do we pass on to young people something true that they can rely on and something beautiful that can sustain their hope? How do we help them know that they belong, that they are loved? Stories are certainly one of the most time-tested and enjoyable ways to go about it.

SLOWING IT DOWN WITH READING DOWN

It might sound counterintuitive, but returning to beloved stories again and again, including ones that we might consider little kid stories, will help children mature into adults of depth and character. I like to think of this as *reading down*. (Not all families are readers, but stick with me, because this principle works for movies and stories you tell by heart, too!)

Reading down means repeating things instead of rushing on to conquer more. Repetition is like meditation; it's a way for kids to chew on a message. As they return to it again and again, the truth and goodness in the story can move from their heads deep down into their hearts. One of the most detrimental effects of having access today to so many things to read, watch, and listen to is the way that variety competes with repetition. A single reading (or viewing) is rarely enough to fully ingest the truth of something. Repetition is at the heart of reading down because it creates familiarity (from the same root word as *family*). Over time, a story becomes a home—a welcome gift to a generation grasping for connectedness.

Not every juvenile book is worth returning to time and again. Reading down is about curating a collection of stories that deserve repeat visits. They might be literary classics, or they might be stories that are special for *you*. What were your favorite books as a child? Something must have set them apart as meaningful for you—perhaps the illustrations, or the characters, or just the bond you formed with the person who read them with you. The stories we have treasured the most with our children often illuminate the sacredness of ordinary daily life—stories about children growing up, or animals on a farm, for example. But our favorites also include books of poetry for children, an alphabet book with classic illustrations, a few epic adventures, and whimsical and humorous storybooks. Beautiful artwork, magnificently crafted words, soul-lifting themes, and laughter administer a powerful dose of hope to the soul. They point the way to the ultimate source of all truth, beauty, and goodness.

Reading down has an altogether different objective from academic reading. There is a time and a place for reading to gain information or to train ourselves for thinking well. But here the objective is to savor stories for their tenderness, hilarity, or encouragement. Too often we set about to conquer a book—even the Good Book—when what we really need is to relax into the posture of one ready to receive a treasure.

One way to practice reading down is to re-create the read-aloud conditions of early childhood for kids of all ages. My parents are in their seventies, but one of their favorite evening activities is to sit by the fire and read great novels to each other. The act of communal story sharing—whether reading from a text or telling a story from memory—creates a sense of belonging and closeness. That relational bonding isn't something kids should have to leave behind just because they're aging up.

Returning to favorite stories and sharing them aloud not only roots kids in their families of origin, but also in the family of God. The Bible narrative was never meant to be a book we finish, accomplish, and check off the list. It's a story to sink into for a lifetime. And the message at the heart of it is that all of us are invited to make a home forever with God and with his people.

In a sense, we are all like the Runaway Bunny as we grow up and venture out into the big world of ideas. But great stories are a home we can always return to.

When I think about the foundations that form in childhood and the many things—like books and stories—that contribute to a child's stability now and in the future, I think about Jesus' words:

> Everyone, then, who hears these words of mine and acts on them will be like a wise man who built his house on rock. The rain fell, the floods came, and the winds blew and beat on that house, but it did not fall because it had been founded on rock. And everyone who hears these words of mine and does not act on them will be like a foolish man who built his house on sand. The rain fell, and the floods came, and the winds blew and beat against that house, and it fell—and great was its fall! (Matthew 7:24-27)

Times of struggle reveal the solidity of the foundation, he explained.

Life is full of pressures and unexpected storms that can shake a person to the core—even to the point of questioning God's presence and love. I want to commend reading down to you—no matter what stage your kids are in, and for you, too—as a practical way to listen to Jesus and recognize moral goodness, to build a sturdy foundation of love and belonging, and to remember that the kingdom of God and his love for us are unshakable.

HOW TO PRACTICE READING DOWN

Most of the ideas I will share with you here came down to me from my parents. My mom is a wonderful storyteller and curator of quality books for kids. I can still remember the way her voice sounded reading certain lines from well-loved books. It's a proud tradition in our family to enjoy reading together. But if you aren't the bookish type, don't worry. I have shared these suggestions with friends and family, and I know they still work when applied to favorite movies, retelling memorable family stories, and even looking through photo albums. The same principles apply: build familiarity through repetition, bond over shared favorites, and highlight what is true and lasting.

1. ***Find a quality children's Bible*** and read it aloud together as a family. I recommend *The Children's Bible in 365 Stories* by Mary Batchelor for a pretty thorough paraphrase. (Wording is geared toward older elementary students.) William has read it with our kids at least four or five times over the past ten years. When I was in seminary, a good children's Bible was actually a recommended resource to help adult students familiarize themselves with the overarching narrative of the Bible. Scripture contains all sorts of genres—poetry, wisdom sayings, history, lists, laws, letters, and so forth. But all of this is set up within the overarching *story* of God-with-people. Sometimes as adults we tend to zoom in on the doctrine-heavy parts of Scripture, or to approach it as a study tool rather than as a story. Each way of reading has its place, but returning to the Bible like a child listening to a wonderful story can be a beautiful way to strengthen your sense of belonging to the family of God and to grow your friendship with Jesus.

2. ***Keep children's books close at hand.*** This is the flipside of the truism "out of sight, out of mind." Keeping kid books on the coffee table or near your desk or on a shelf by the bed might encourage you or your kids to pick one up and thumb through it from time to time. If you aren't reading to a child, you might feel uncomfortable just sitting down and cracking open an illustrated children's book, but you shouldn't! Think of it as a little tour down memory lane.

3. *Book clubs, book buddies, and family reads.* If you take in books, movies, and listening mostly on your own, this could be a helpful aspect of the reading down principle to zoom in on. *Sharing* stories is the best way to get the most out of them and form deep bonds by sharing the memories. I recommend reading aloud with your kids, joining a book club, or finding a reading buddy to discuss with. The story then becomes the meeting place around which memories and connections can form. Shared viewing of movies can be a connection point, too, but stories told orally by loved ones hold special significance.

4. *A few suggestions divided by age:*

Toddlers and preschoolers

- Take note of stories, songs, and nursery rhymes that your child seems particularly drawn to at an early age. Returning to these over and over again will turn them into shared connections. My kids still remember the ones we repeated the most!

- Buy an extra copy of favorite books and tuck one away in case it goes out of print. Trust me, your shelf copy is going to get a lot of love, and having a backup can come in handy!

- Stick to human and animal characters and concrete, everyday storylines with clear ties to a child's day-to-day reality. It is important for little ones to form a solid understanding about how the world works before dipping into abstract or fantasy plots.

Elementary age

- Look for narratives with engaging plots. Fact books are great, but they can have an overwhelming amount of data, and some kids fixate on the enormity of it. Plus narratives convey truth in a way that pure facts can't.

- Write inscriptions in the front of books that you want to highlight for your child. A special message inside shows that this is a book worth returning to.

- If you're trying to build a child's literacy skills, the most important thing is to make reading enjoyable. Reading below grade level gives a sense of mastery and takes frustration out of the equation. Even if it isn't stretching new vocabulary, it's helping your child have positive associations with the act of reading and continuing to ground them in the benefits of truth and belonging.

Older kids and teenagers (It's not too late to start, or revive, reading down)

- Tell stories from your kid's childhood around the dinner table or in the car and at special occasions. These shared narratives will fortify their sense of belonging—even if they roll their eyes.

- Use a rainy day or a holiday as an occasion to pull out the young reader books. Let each family member pick one off the shelf that they remember from when they were little and read it or tell everyone something they remember about it. My kids are twelve and fifteen now, and they love doing this!

- Gift older kids a children's book that holds a special memory (for them, or for you) each birthday to start a growing collection of favorites. Let them know you aren't saying they are babies, but that everyone deserves to have a collection of classics.

- If a child feels insulted by the idea of reading baby books, find a way to frame reading down as a service to younger siblings, cousins, neighbors, or friends. They'll think that they're doing it for the sake of the little kid, but they'll be soaking in the goodness as well. Great stories can even sink into hard ground.

- As kids read up and engage in youth and young adult books, just be very selective. There is a lot of junk out there.

In our intellectual ambitions and our attempts to be all grown up and free, we often form grand plans for launching out into the unknown. God meets us there, of course, but he also calls us home.

Augustine prayed, "You have made us for yourself, O Lord, and our heart is restless until it rests in you."

Stories (and the forms that contain them—books, movies, and oral traditions) are rich repositories of truth and reminders of who and whose we are. Isn't it funny that God so often reveals himself in places we overlook—a simple children's book, a family memory, an illustration that speaks volumes to our hearts? In returning to time-tested and beautifully crafted words, and in sharing them with the dear ones in your care, may you find a growing familiarity with God, with each other, and with everything good.

19

Counterpoints

ON A FAMILY VACATION to the Northeast one spring, we took the kids to see a Scout camp just outside of New York City. Driving out of the boroughs and over the bridge, the billboards and traffic gradually subsided, and a 143-acre oasis appeared.

A light rain was falling as an elderly camp patron gave my family a little off-season tour of the property. He showed us cabins and a lake, and he told us a bit about the troops from the city that come here for retreat.

Even though the camp was only twenty miles from the heart of Manhattan, it felt like the middle of nowhere. The environment here, in contrast to the bustling life of the city we had just left, was a welcome relief. We had spent the past few days sightseeing in New York with little children, and we were all a bit overstimulated and in need of a break. It was nice to come away to a spot with so few people and so few manmade things. No cars honking, no intrusive screens and speakers. Even the colors were pared down from the shiny steel and neon signs of the city.

I imagined that the peace and tranquility of this place must be a huge gift to city kids. I said so to our guide. He agreed, but he said that most of the kids are really tense when they first arrive, even frightened by the change. "If you've never experienced silence before, it can come as quite a shock," he explained. "It takes about forty-eight hours for the kids to relax and begin to enjoy everything that is here for them. But they need it. They sure do need it."

IMBALANCE AND AVOIDANCE

The old man's observation has stuck with me. Sharp imbalances in modern lifestyles divert children away from experiences and relationships that feed and refresh their souls; even worse, prolonged imbalances can actually cause kids to fear or avoid what they most need. The overscheduled child, for example, becomes so accustomed to busyness that he might eventually feel quite panicked if there's nothing going on.

If you look at the typical patterns in children's lives right now, you can observe this trend:

- too much noise → fear of silence
- too much entertainment → discomfort with boredom
- too much augmented virtual reality → dissatisfaction with reality
- too much digital interaction → awkwardness in face-to-face interactions
- too much time inside → dislike for the outdoors
- too much isolation → apprehension about being known
- too much public visibility → fear of being unknown
- too much force → disdain for gentleness
- too much newness → avoidance of repetition

In each of these examples (and there are many others we could name), too much of one thing leads to habitual avoidance of its opposite, and it carves a deeper and deeper chasm between children and the environments and experiences that could restore balance and wholeness to their growing-up years. Incongruencies in childhood eventually harden into adult dysfunction.

Worst of all, the lopsided experience so common for many children today triggers fear and avoidance of things that naturally point young people to God and allow them to calm down enough to discover that he is present, active, and responsive. C. S. Lewis once wrote that avoiding God is "extremely easy" in the modern world—simply, "Avoid silence, avoid solitude, avoid any train of thought that leads off the

beaten track. . . . Keep the radio on. Live in a crowd. Use plenty
of sedation."

By naming these common avoidances, Lewis reveals the antidote.
The experiences that children avoid often are exactly what they need in
order to thrive. For example, helping kids step into peaceful, quiet—like
the Scout camp's wilderness environment—is a timely antidote to a wide-
spread problem (excessive noise). But quiet is just one of many contrasts
that this generation needs. For children to have a spacious, God-soaked
childhood, they need access to all the fertile environments, activities,
and relationships that lie on the opposite extreme of our modern compulsions. Spotting and correcting imbalances in our kids' lives is a discerning and corrective process that I like to call *counterpoints*.

SLOWING IT DOWN WITH COUNTERPOINTS

Jesus was no stranger to the perils of imbalance. He knew that even
good things—without contrast—can disrupt the soul's equilibrium and
distance us from our heavenly Father. During his years of intense
public ministry, Jesus regularly withdrew to catch his breath. And he
invited his friends to join him. "Come away to a deserted place all by
yourselves and rest a while" (Mark 6:31). He understood that a con-
trasting environment or activity can be an oasis in a spiritual desert,
an abundant place of rest and connection with God.

We can imitate Jesus' invitational posture, calling kids to come away
from whatever has become too much and to find the counterpoints
that their souls need. When I taught at an elementary school, I knew
that my students did lots of desk and computer work in their other
classes. I wanted to offer them a counterpoint in my class. So we sat on
the rug in a circle and connected face-to-face, and I incorporated art,
music, and storytelling to draw them into our Bible lessons and discussions about God. Providing kids with contrast helps to keep small imbalances from hardening into habitual forms of avoidance and fear.

Counterpoints are not always comfortable, but they are necessary and good. Experiencing boredom, solitude, and face-to-face

engagement can push kids (and grown-ups) outside their comfort zones, which doesn't feel very much like savoring. Even when the contrast is well-timed, appropriate, and wise, there will be resistance. As the Scout camp guide pointed out to me, even a wonderful infusion of what a soul needs can be quite jarring at first. The greater the need for the contrast, the more shocking it is to the system. But like plunging into a pool of water on a hot day, it's a shock that soothes, restores, and refreshes.

A jarring contrast can be good for the soul, but counterpoints aren't about fanaticism. It's tempting to take drastic measures when we realize our children's lives are off-kilter. But rushing to solutions may just be trading one extreme for another and usually leads to more imbalance. In most cases, the better approach is to make subtle, slow adjustments. We can lead our kids into the refreshing waters of contrast without going off the deep end. For example, too much activity needs the counterpoint of downtime. But if we swap all activity for rest, we will have gone too far. Although Jesus sought solitude in the wilderness, he wasn't *always* alone. He had a very public-facing role proclaiming the good news, healing, and teaching. Can you see that this is more of a both-and than an either-or?

While we need to avoid extremism, I don't mean to suggest that counterpoints are a kind of yin-yang unity of opposites. There are some things that do not belong in childhood. Period. For example, I mentioned in a previous chapter that I believe the right amount of social media for my kids during childhood is zero. We don't need to add it to our lives just for the sake of contrast. The main objective isn't forces in opposition or even balance as an end in itself, but rather *wholeness*—for the sake of a vibrant, deep life with God and people. Over time, as we facilitate counterpoints for our children that allow them to experience a childhood to the full, without gaping holes or excesses, they will begin to recognize what is good for their souls. And they will be more likely to return to the oasis, even if they wander from it when they first strike out independently.

Counterpoints

HOW TO PRACTICE COUNTERPOINTS

We can apply the principle of contrast to any number of situations, but first, let me share with you a few counterpoints that I have used as a parent and as a teacher.

1. ***Solitude spots.*** I am a big believer in prescribing alone time for kids, even very young kids. The point is not to hush them or just to get a little breathing space for yourself (although that's nice too!). The point is to help them learn to be comfortable alone, because alone time supports attention to God. When the kids were very young, solitude looked different. I would play with them for a bit and get them going with a craft, pretend game, book, etc., and then say, "You keep going for a little bit by yourself." They wouldn't always comply, but gradually they learned to be okay on their own in their rooms for stretches at a time.

   Sometimes it helps to designate a special spot at home or school or church where kids can withdraw for solitude and silence. This could be a fort that a child builds, or a calm and cozy reading nook, or a whole room dedicated as a distraction-free zone. Involve kids in the design and construction of the space so that they are learning to choose and shape environments that refresh their souls.

   Because we're talking about balance, it's important to note that not all kids are starved for solitude and silence. Isolation is an oppressive form of solitude—much of it the result of isolating technologies. Warm, embodied, community interactions that put them face-to-face with friends might be uncomfortable, but it's an important counterpoint for kids struggling with isolation.

2. ***Boredom.*** Too many toys, too much entertainment, and too much reliance on someone to facilitate are typical imbalances for kids today. The best recipe I know for stirring up play is boredom. One example from a few years back: On a rainy day, after a fair amount of whining and bickering, the kids finally

came up with something to do. They gathered all the baskets, trash cans, and buckets they could find around the house and arranged them up and down the stairs in a pinball-like maze. The object of the game was to bounce a ball down the stairs and avoid certain containers while landing in others. There was an elaborate scoring system that I didn't fully understand—but that didn't matter because I wasn't playing or supervising. The next time there is a lull—maybe a day off school, or a rainy afternoon— try saying no screens and taking a hands-off approach. The empty space becomes the soil in which imagination, ingenuity, and resourcefulness can grow.

3. *The power of a whisper.* Did you know that if a crowd is very boisterous and you want to get their attention, adding to the volume by trying to speak louder is unlikely to work? This is something I first learned from my mom. The best approach is to get very, very quiet, so that others have to hush to hear you. I once knew a brilliant preschool teacher who would do this. She was the gentlest little woman—so gentle I didn't think she would be able to handle the students. But whenever she addressed the children, she would get down on their level and speak in her hushed, calm way, and the preschoolers would all gather around her and perk up their ears. Whether it is a literal whisper or some other mild way of interacting, the contrast of gentleness is a refuge for children who are too quickly exposed to force, frenzy, and manipulation. And it helps to shape kids into people who can interact publicly with a gentle yet powerful, Christlike presence.

Counterpoints aren't a one-size-fits-all prescription. The right balance between time spent in solitude and time spent in company, for example, will be unique for every child just as it is for every adult. How then are we to know what is needed? If there is no formula, how will we know if our children have too much of something or too little? And if we do detect imbalances, how will we know what counterpoints to use? The answer is discernment. And discernment is listening to God. The Good Shepherd will gladly help us make wise decisions on our children's behalf if we pay attention.

So as you seek his guidance in finding the right pace for you and your child, be a good listener.

Listen to your life. If we pay attention, God will highlight things that reveal his heart's desire for young people—snippets from family life, conversations with wise teachers and friends, truths that jump off the page of great books, memories from your own childhood. God often uses our memories as sacred beacons to illuminate his own perspective. Listen for clues about what's too fast, what needs to slow down, and other imbalances that need a counterpoint.

Listen to each other. Discuss your observations and questions with your friends and family. I believe sharing our stories in community lights the path and makes our journey more enjoyable than if we go it alone.

Listen to the life of Jesus. Going slowly through the Gospels always surfaces new insight. Jesus' interactions with people and their ways of interacting with him hold a wealth of wisdom for how to live the gently paced life of loving God and savoring all that he is doing in us and in the world.

Listen to the Holy Spirit in prayer. The most important conversation for you to continue is the one between you and the Lord. Listening to God for inspiration and encouragement is essential in this hard work. Reflecting with the Spirit on each day's experiences—both positive and negative. What was too much or too fast for your kids today? Or for you? Where did you experience calm, gratitude, peace? Seeking God's perspective on these noticings is the only way to ensure that we don't power ahead in our own strength, our own timing, and our own ideas about what to change. Listening prayer can be private, but it can also be communal. Pray with your child, your spouse, your family members, your church, and others who share your longing for kids to have the life God intended.

Benediction

THIS BOOK HAS TAKEN SHAPE around the edges of family life and a full-time job.

I had foolishly fantasized about writing it from some kind of retreat setting—maybe a solitary cottage on a remote Scottish island. It is a good thing that idea turned out to be financially and logistically impossible because that scenario would have been ridiculously incompatible with my purpose for this book: to help normal people take realistic steps—today, in their homes and classrooms and churches—to push back on the frenzy of modern living. How could I give anyone practical advice for slowing down to savor childhood unless I remain fully embedded in my family's life while I write?

So here I am, putting the final words on this book not from a getaway in Scotland, but from my own home, where there are clothes to fold and meals to cook and family games to play, and where I am about to go upstairs and kiss my kids goodnight.

Writing this book has made our life together busier in some ways. I had to miss out on some things, and I know my kids are ready for me to be finished. But by adjusting things along the way I was able to slow down enough to help with homework, paint fingernails, celebrate birthdays, play board games, and join in for episodes of *All Creatures Great and Small*. If my family can savor childhood, yours can too.

Even in the midst of the challenges we all face in our modern fast-paced world, small steps to slow down make it possible for kids (and grown-ups!) to have wholesome experiences, rooted relationships, and an ever-deepening life with God.

If you are still digesting what we have covered in *Savoring Childhood*—and we've covered a lot—don't rush on. Circle back. Reread. Keep letting little insights work their way from your head into your actual living and doing.

Be encouraged! You are already closer than you were before you started. And remember, God is with us on this journey. "May the grace of the Lord Jesus Christ, and the love of God, and the fellowship of the Holy Spirit be with you all" (2 Corinthians 13:13).

PRAYING PSALM 23 FOR OUR CHILDREN

Psalm 23 is one of the world's most beloved images of life at a gentle pace. It is a picture of human flourishing that holds true for all of us, old and young. The Good Shepherd leads the way to the encounters and environments that feed and refresh the soul, and the Good Shepherd fends off danger. In his paths, under his care, a person can be full to overflowing with joy and goodness and completely at home in the Lord's presence, despite challenges.

The Shepherd sets a pattern for our care for young people. What can we learn from him? What can we ask him to help us with?

Try this: Using Psalm 23 as your outline, expand it with your own words to shape it into a personal prayer for the child who is on your heart. Write in the book if you like, or write on other paper.

Slowly go through the familiar psalm below, and add specific names (such as, "The Lord is Charlotte's shepherd . . .") and other details. Name some of the good things your child needs in order to flourish. Specify, if you can, the dark valleys they may have to walk through. List some marks of wisdom and character you hope to see forming in your child's unique personality.

As you personalize the psalm, picture lifting your child into the Good Shepherd's care, so that everything is paced just right for their souls to be fully alive. Your prayers, combined with your small steps to resist the pressure to go too fast, will do more, with God's help, than you can imagine.

The LORD is my shepherd; I shall not want.

He makes me lie down in green pastures;
he leads me beside still waters;
he restores my soul.

He leads me in right paths
for his name's sake.

Even though I walk through the darkest valley,
I fear no evil;
for you are with me;
your rod and your staff,
they comfort me.

You prepare a table before me
in the presence of my enemies;
you anoint my head with oil;
my cup overflows.

Surely goodness and mercy shall follow me
all the days of my life,
and I shall dwell in the house of the LORD
my whole life long.

Acknowledgments

THANKS BE TO GOD for bringing this book into existence. Every good thought is from him. Every open door to publication has come to me as grace upon grace. "To him be the glory and the power for ever and ever. Amen" (1 Peter 4:11).

I also want to say a heartfelt thank-you to:

My parents, Toni and Charlie Pate, who read early drafts and cheered me on. Mom touched every single page in the book with her editor's pen, asking excellent questions, offering suggestions, and drawing hearts in the margin. Mom and Dad, most of the wisdom in this book is from you. Thank you for giving me a loving, playful childhood with spiritual depth and moral beauty.

Family (siblings, in-laws, grandparents, cousins, aunts, uncles, and extended family) and church family who cheered me on. Thank you for your encouragement and practical support along the way.

Friends who listened to me go on and on about the ideas in this book and asked me how it was going. A special thanks to those who read bits and pieces and helped me work through some writing decisions: Melody Leeper, Monty Harrington, Katelyn Dixon, Dawn King, Nathan and Vivianne Foster, and Catherine Darling. Park and Terry Smith and Jeanie Hoover read the unedited manuscript and offered detailed comments on everything from theology, to writing craft, to the point of view of grandparents. Thank you for this labor of love!

Renovaré colleagues, who celebrated and prayed with me: Brian, Monty, Kim, Carolyn, Mel, Wendy, Kasey, Brandan, Ted, and Kevin. And mentors who talked with me about ideas in the very early stages and affirmed my writing: Chris Hall, Richard Foster, and Lacy Borgo.

My editor, Cindy Bunch, who sparked the concept for *Savoring Childhood* and gave me the opportunity to write it. And the rest of the InterVarsity Press team—thank you all for caring about childhood and making this book possible!

My amazing kids, Charlotte and Henry, who gave me permission to talk about our family's life. They shared their perspectives with me so that I could represent the typical conditions of modern childhood as accurately as possible. Kids, y'all are sensitive, kind, thoughtful, and creative. Daddy and I are so proud of you. Henry, thank you for listening to me read aloud from chapters and laughing to make me feel funny. Charlotte, thank you for making me snacks and helping around the house so that I could keep writing when the deadlines hit. And thank you, Charlotte, for the wonderful illustrations!

Most of all my husband William, who read and reread every page. He is my closest collaborator—in this book and in the adventure of parenting. He is often my teacher in savoring childhood. He made my writing better by suggesting cuts, polishing sentences. He took hundreds of walks with me during the writing of this book and listened with Christlike patience while I talked through the ideas in my head. William, you are wise. I love you.

Notes

PART 1: SLOW GRATIFICATION

7   *superficiality*: Richard Foster, *Celebration of Discipline: The Path to Spiritual Growth* (HarperSanFrancisco, 1998), 1.
    deeply formed life: Rich Villodas, *The Deeply Formed Life: Five Transformative Values to Root Us in the Way of Jesus* (WaterBrook, 2020).

1. SWEET COUNTDOWNS

10   *youthness of youth*: Eugenia Pearson Curry, "The Magic of Expectancy," unpublished manuscript [1940-1960].

11   *Veruca Salt*: *Willy Wonka and the Chocolate Factory*, directed by Mel Stuart (1971).

2. STRETCHING

18   *US families struggle:* Jeffrey C. Fuhrer, "Forty-three Percent of All Families in the U. S. Fall Short of Meeting Basic Needs," Brookings, June 20, 2024, www.brookings.edu/articles/how-many-are-in-need-in-the-us-the-poverty-rate-is-the-tip-of-the-iceberg/.

19   *every discipline*: Dallas Willard, "A Picture of the Disciplined: Freedom and Submission," transcript of teaching from Woodlake Avenue Friends Church, May 26, 1974, www.conversatio.org/a-picture-of-the-disciplined-freedom-and-submission.

3. TIME MACHINES

29   *old model*: Wendell Berry, *What Are People For?: Essays* (Counterpoint, 1990), 170–71.
    For a Student: Joseph Fasano, "For a Student Who Used AI to Write a Paper" from *The Last Song of the World* (BOA Editions Ltd., www.boa editions.org, 2024). Used by permission.

30   *omnipresent technology use*: Peco and Ruth Gaskovski, "Sowing Anachronism: How to be Weird in Public, and Private: Flip Phones, Dip Ink, Vespers, and Other Time Machines," Substack, December 6, 2023, https://schooloftheunconformed.substack.com/p/sowing-anachronism-how-to-be-weird.

31   *Luddite Club*: Alex Vadukul, "These 'Luddite' Teens Are Abstaining from Social Media," *The New York Times*, December 15, 2022, www .nytimes.com/2022/12/15/style/teens-social-media.html.

34   *savoring the hours*: Carl Honoré, *In Praise of Slow: How a Worldwide Movement Is Challenging the Cult of Speed* (Vintage Canada, 2004).

4. LONG-TERM PROJECTS

39   *instant society*: Eugene Peterson, *A Long Obedience in the Same Direction: Discipleship in an Instant Society* (InterVarsity Press, 2024), title page.

5. A PALACE IN TIME

53   *palace in time*: Abraham Joshua Heschel, *The Sabbath: Its Meaning for Modern Man* (Farrar, Straus & Giroux, 2005), chapter 1.
       keeping things out: Marva Dawn, *A Royal Waste of Time* (Eerdmans, 1999), 217-22.

54   *something of value*: Dallas Willard, "Disciplines of Abstinence and Engagement" (lecture, African Enterprise, South Africa, May 1985), https:// conversatio.org/the-disciplines-of-abstinence-and-engagement-secrecy -sacrifice/.

55   *sacred assembly*: Leviticus 23:3. The word *synagogue* comes from a Greek verb that means "to gather together."

56   *interlude:* Heschel, *The Sabbath*, 14.

6. TIDYING UP

63   *tidying up*: Marie Kondo, *The Life-Changing Magic of Tidying Up: The Japanese Art of Decluttering and Organizing* (Clarkson Potter/Ten Speed, 2014).

64   *how we spend our days*: Annie Dillard, *The Writing Life* (Harper Perennial, 1989), 32.

71   *ruthlessly eliminate hurry:* Dallas Willard in John Ortberg, *Soul Keeping: Caring for the Most Important Part of You* (Zondervan, 2014), 20.

7. SPEED CHECKS

76   *reality of motion*: Joseph Mazur, "Feeling Fast Feeling," *Psychology Today*, November 22, 2020, www.psychologytoday.com/us/blog/the -speed-of-life/202011/feeling-fast-feeling (emphasis mine).

8. SINGLETASKING

83   *first act of love*: Dallas Willard, *The Spirit of the Disciplines: Understanding How God Changes Lives* (HarperCollins, 1991), 210.

84 *frontal cortex*: Ellen Barlow, "Under the Hood of the Adolescent Brain," *Harvard Medical School News*, October, 2014, https://hms .harvard.edu/news/under-hood-adolescent-brain.

85 *develop executive functions*: "InBrief: Executive Function: Skills for Life and Learning," Center on the Developing Child, Harvard University, May 20, 2012, https://developingchild.harvard.edu/wp-content/uploads /2024/10/InBrief-Executive-Function-Skills-for-Life-and-Learning -2.pdf.

9. OFFLOADING

95 *The Crown*, season 6, episode 5, "Willsmania," written by Peter Morgan, Jonathan Wilson, and Meriel Sheibani-Clare, directed by May el-Toukhy, aired December 14, 2023, on Netflix.

96 *192 alerts per day*: Jonathan Haidt, *The Anxious Generation: How the Great Rewiring of Childhood Is Causing an Epidemic of Mental Illness* (Penguin Random House, 2024), 126.

97 *I participated in a group chat*: Lara D'Entremont, "Does Your Online Life Leave You Too Depleted for Local Community?" *A Mother Held* (blog), Substack, March 18, 2024, https://laradentremont.substack .com/p/does-your-online-life-leave-you-too.

10. SNAIL MAIL

107 *drown us in shallow content*: Marshall McLuhan, *Understanding Media: The Extensions of Man* (McGraw-Hill, 1964); Neil Postman, *Amusing Ourselves to Death: Public Discourse in the Age of Show Business* (Viking, 1985).

109 *more pleasing to me*: Cicero, *The Letters of Cicero*, ed. Evelyn S. Shuck-burgh (George Bell and Sons, 1908–1909).

11. LIBRARY CARTS

116 *concentration, contemplation, and reflection*: Nicholas Carr, *The Shallows: What the Internet Is Doing to Our Brains* (W. W. Norton & Company, 2010), marketing copy.
illusion of completeness: Therese Fessenden, "Scrolling and Attention," NN/g, April 15, 2018, www.nngroup.com/articles/scrolling-and-attention/.

116 *long-term memory and recall*: Betsy Sparrow et al., "Google Effects on Memory: Cognitive Consequences of Having Information at Our Fin-gertips," *Science* 333, 776–78 (2011), DOI:10.1126/science.1207745.

117 *mental health crisis*: Jonathan Haidt, "Four Foundational Harms," *The Anxious Generation* (Penguin, 2024).

121 L. Altamura, C. Vargas, and L. Salmerón, "Do New Forms of Reading
     Pay Off? A Meta-Analysis on the Relationship Between Leisure Digital
     Reading Habits and Text Comprehension," *Review of Educational Re-
     search*, *95*(1), 2023 (original work published 2025), 53-88.

12. RECORD PLAYERS

128 *intimate with our technology*: Marva Dawn, *Unfettered Hope: A Call to
     Faithful Living in an Affluent Society* (Westminster, 2003), 167.

PART 4: SLOW CONSUMING

133 *throwaway culture*: Francis, *Laudato Si* (Encyclical Letter on Care for
     Our Common Home), the Holy See, May 24, 2015, www.vatican.va
     /content/francesco/en/encyclicals/documents/papa-francesco_20150524
     _enciclica-laudato-si.html.

13. SIMPLE TASTES

138 *nervousness and fury of acquisitiveness*: Abraham Joshua Heschel, *The
     Sabbath: Its Meaning for Modern Man* (Farrar, Straus & Giroux, 2005), 1.
     given our hearts away: William Wordsworth, "The World Is Too Much
     With Us," 1807, public domain.

14. THE CREATIVE OPTION

147 *merit badges*: Ted Gioia, "How to Break Free from Dopamine Culture,"
     The Honest Broker (blog), Substack, March 4, 2024, www.honest-broker
     .com/p/how-to-break-free-from-dopamine-culture.

148 *nothing to live for*: Katherine Sellgren, "Young People 'Feel They Have
     Nothing to Live For,'" BBC (January 2, 2014), www.bbc.com/news
     /education-25559089.
     bombarded with b***s**t: Eli George and Jon Haidt, "Do the Kids Think
     They're Alright?," *After Babel*, Substack, April 12, 2023, www.afterbabel
     .com/p/do-the-kids-think-theyre-alright.
     creators, initiators, not just receivers: Luci Shaw, "Spiritual Disciplines in
     a Postmodern World: An Interview of Dallas Willard," *Radix*, Vol. 27, No. 2.
     continual vision: Richard Foster, *Streams of Living Water* (Harper-
     Collins, 2010), 250.
     the work of our hands: Foster, *Streams*, 249.

15. HEARTFELT GIFTS

157 *rein it in with the toys*: Bryan Jarrell, "The Tyranny of Toys: A Gift
     Giving Guide from Parents Everywhere," *Mockingbird*, December 11,
     2024, https://mbird.com/everyday/the-tyranny-of-toys/.

158   *love languages*: Gary Chapman, *The 5 Love Languages: The Secret to Love that Lasts* (Northfield Publishing, 2014).

16. REVIVAL SKILLS

166   *to hasten obsolescence*: Peter Mommsen, "Living in Praise of Repair Culture," *Plough*, December 4, 2023, www.plough.com/en/topics/justice /sustainable-living/in-praise-of-repair-culture.
      quickening replacement cycle: Mommsen, "Living in Praise of Repair Culture."
167   *marketing to kids*: Laura Ordoñez, "How Influencers Wield Marketing Power Over Kids," Common Sense Media, May 1, 2024, www.common sensemedia.org/kids-action/articles/how-influencers-wield-marketing -power-over-kids.

17. ANIMAL FRIENDS

180   *God wants to be seen*: Julian of Norwich, *Revelations of Divine Love*, trans. Grace Warrack (Christian Ethereal Classics, 1901), https://ccel.org /ccel/julian/revelations/revelations.

18. READING DOWN

189   *If you become a bird:* Margaret Wise Brown and Clement Hurd, *The Runaway Bunny* (Harper, 1942).
190   *deep people*: Richard Foster, *Celebration of Discipline: The Path to Spiritual Growth* (HarperSanFrancisco, 1998), 1.
191   *We rely on all these experts:* Freya India, "We Need Moral Direction," *Girls* (blog), Substack, August 13, 2024, www.freyaindia.co.uk/p /we-need-moral-direction.
      The problem is: India, "Moral Direction."
197   *until it rests in you*: Augustine of Hippo, *Confessions*, 1,1.5, public domain.

19. COUNTERPOINTS

199   *avoid silence, avoid solitude*: C. S. Lewis, "The Seeing Eye," *Christian Reflections*, ed. Walter Hooper (Eerdmans, 1995), 168-69.
204   *sacred beacons*: Frederick Buechner, *Listening to Your Life* (HarperOne, 1992), 232.

ivp formatio

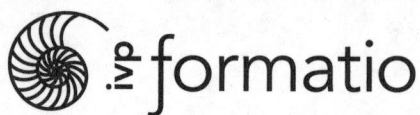

BECOMING OUR TRUE SELVES

The nautilus is one of the sea's oldest creatures. Beginning with a tight center, its remarkable growth pattern can be seen in the ever-enlarging chambers that spiral outward. The nautilus in the IVP Formatio logo symbolizes deep inward work of spiritual formation that begins rooted in our souls and then opens to the world as we experience spiritual transformation. The shell takes on a stunning pearlized appearance as it ages and forms in much the same way as the souls of those who devote themselves to spiritual practice. Formatio books draw on the ancient wisdom of the saints and the early church as well as the rich resources of Scripture, applying tradition to the needs of contemporary life and practice.

Within each of us is a longing to be in God's presence. Formatio books call us into our deepest desires and help us to become our true selves in the light of God's grace.

LIKE THIS BOOK?

Scan the code to discover more content like this!

Get on IVP's email list to receive special offers, exclusive book news, and thoughtful content from your favorite authors on topics you care about.

IVPRESS.COM/BOOK-QR